SHE'S GOT NEXT

SHE'S GOT NEXT

A STORY
OF GETTING IN,
STAYING OPEN,
AND TAKING A SHOT

Melissa King

A MARINER ORIGINAL
HOUGHTON MIFFLIN COMPANY
Boston • New York • 2005

For information about permission to reproduce selections
from this book, write to Permissions, Houghton Mifflin Company,
215 Park Avenue South, New York, New York 10003.

Visit our Web site: www.houghtonmifflinbooks.com.

Library of Congress Cataloging-in-Publication Data
King, Melissa.
   She's got next : a story of getting in, staying open, and taking a shot
   / Melissa King.
      p.   cm.
   "A Mariner original."
   ISBN 0-618-26456-6
   1. Basketball — United States. 2. Urban youth — Recreation
   — United States. 3. King, Melissa. I. Title.
   GV885.4.K56 2005
   796.323'092 — dc22 [B] 2004062756

Book design by Melissa Lotfy

Printed in the United States of America

MP 10 9 8 7 6 5 4 3 2 1

This is a book of nonfiction. However, readers should be
aware that the author has made an effort to arrange these
contents artfully. Overall, as nearly as possible, the particulars
may have been disguised to protect anonymity but have not
been otherwise altered.

Portions of this book were published previously, in slightly
different form, in the *Chicago Reader* and *Sport Literate*.

For Jackson

Acknowledgments

WITH THANKS to my editor, Susan Canavan, for her high standards, and my agent, Stella Connell, for her unwavering loyalty and professionalism. To friends and family members Scot Danforth, Andy King, Deb King, Lee King, Garry Powell, Kevin Pritchett, Adam Ritchey, and Steve Wilson, who read drafts and always encouraged. To the members of the Northwest Arkansas Community Writers' Guild, for their readings and friendship. To Laura Hohnhold of The Editor's Room, for her thoughtful comments. To Glenn Stout and Richard Ford, for including the Chicago stories in *Best American Sports Writing 1999,* and to Alison True, for publishing these stories in the *Chicago Reader.* Finally, and most of all, I want to thank the players.

Contents

SHE'S GOT NEXT

Warm Up

STRANGE, how it is with some things you always look for, how you can go around with your channels set. Me, I pick up a flash of orange roundness, a repetitive bouncing *thunk* so purely noticeable whether it's disappearing quickly into the sky or echoing off walls and ceilings. I keep looking for that orange, that *thunk*, because finding it feels like a dive into forgetting.

A new ball, its leather smooth and aromatic, or an old junker with skin as rough as carpenters' hands, it doesn't matter, whether the nets are ragged or missing altogether or rainwater rests in the dips of the concrete or your dribble comes off funny from the floor's hollow spots, doesn't matter.

Basketball. I've played anytime, anywhere, with anyone I can, until I was too tired to stand or everyone had gone home. I've played because I need to move, forget myself, prove that the world can be different. I've played because, when the game is good, when everyone is doing, not thinking, it happens, little stillnesses in the moments when you see your open man and nothing else, or you feel your shot going in the hoop as it leaves your hands, or you share a laugh with someone you've never spoken to. Race, money, gender, age, they're still there. But the junk we're all saddled with is gone. You can see its absence in the other players' faces, hear its sorry ass departed in their voices, feel it leaving yourself, if only for a few blessed moments.

When the game ends, the world that's called the real one is back, a lot more suddenly than you'd ever think it would be. You go home and come to play another day with whoever's around, their channels set like yours, ready to dive.

I think it matters, all those ragtag games.

Away Games

IMAGINE a gangly and freckled Arkansas girl, spending her abundant free time picking wild blackberries along dirt roads, cursing the chigger, and perfecting a toad catch-and-release program.

That was me. Sometimes I'd throw cats in my grandparents' pond, just to see if they could swim. They could, but I still feel bad about it.

There were no flute lessons or gymnastics classes or swimming at the park or YMCAs in my world. Most families' social lives revolved around church, but ours didn't. Instead, I had intimate knowledge of wild fruit and invisible parasites and toads stained the same rust color as the sharp, rocky ground no match for the soles of my bare feet. And a basketball hoop at the edge of our driveway, where my younger brother Andy and I spent hour after hour in an area of concrete the size of an El Camino and a Grand Prix parked side by side. Sometimes Andy's friends or my dad joined us. We played two-on-two, three-on-three, two-on-three when we had to.

Hands on a ball, ball in a net, one body blocking the way of another: things were good in the driveway. You fouled, that was a walk, good defense, way to hustle, you're out, nice rebound. It was the pleasant talk, the rules, unchoreographed yet somehow synchronized movement, the desire to find your teammate's strengths, anticipate what he might do next, and help him do it. And there was my dad's smile, too. I relaxed when I saw it.

It seemed important to make good grades and go to college, and so that's what I did until I found myself graduated and working as a copywriter at a land development company. By most standards, this was a relatively unremarkable setup, but it was a big jump for the gangly girl whose parents had married at nineteen, quickly had two babies, and spent the next twenty years recovering.

It was a good job, with a desk and air conditioning and everything. But, ignorant and college-educated as I was, I was burdened by the idea that it was all supposed to *mean* something. When my vision began to blur at the sight of my blank computer screen, I nurtured a dream of being somewhere else, anywhere else, doing anything other than using the written word to convince midwesterners that what they needed more than anything was a half-acre retirement home site nestled in the majestic beauty of the Ozark Mountains.

Surely it had something to do with living in the state whose informal motto was "Thank God for Mississippi." Surely any person could become depressed and have her eyes glaze over all the time when success meant coming in next-to-last in national poverty, teenage pregnancy, education, teeth per capita, or just about anything else you'd care to measure. Surely this was the explanation for my disinterest in implementing and organizing and going forward at my job. Or much of anything else everyone seemed so wild about, while I was on the subject. It was Arkansas's fault.

In another state, a real city, work would be interesting and worthwhile. My boss would be a gifted leader who made it impossible not to be enamored with my job. In this place, women who were my friends would definitely not have pet horses in their yards, jumping like gigantic dogs to greet the mistress of the house as she drove up in her pickup truck. In the city, I would spend my time with liberated, sophisticated females who were much like Dorothy Parker in appearance and demeanor. And the men! They would be everywhere, a buffet of colors and types. Surprisingly, given the fascinating diversity of this group, every single one of them would have in common a preference for the Dorothy Parkers of the world and would not describe opinionated women as smart-alecky or a royal pain in the ass.

I began looking for somewhere cold, expensive, and the setting for at least one violent television show, and after a few months of searching, I found a new good job at a natural foods company in Chicago. When I backed my overflowing Honda out of the driveway and pointed it north, my grandmother's plaintive "Oh, honey, why?" was still fresh in my ears.

And the answer was, at twenty-seven years old, I craved a new intimate knowledge of reality as defined by me. And "real" wasn't any Chicago neighborhood where shirtless young clean-cut guys jogged tanly in pairs down the sidewalk, where people watched ball games from rooftops, or where signs protected empty street parking meant only for those cars bearing the neighborhood sticker. Such sights gave me a powerful feeling of loneliness, from the outside, where the good life of the young professional seemed so self-conscious and proud of itself, like a machine that took in twenty-somethings, mixed them all together, and spit them out paired into suburbs.

Arkansas had its version of that. Everywhere must have its version of that.

My Chicago was walking up the street to get a slice, because I'd seen that in a Spike Lee movie, never mind that this was Chicago and not New York. It was knowing where to put the money when I got on the bus. It was getting yelled at, and yelling right back. Had I been shot at going in the front door of my ancient, destined-for-demolition walkup on the near West Side, I would have ducked the bullets and started humming "If My Friends Could See Me Now."

It's a wonder I wasn't killed.

When I returned to Chicago after visits to Arkansas, I was always glad to be back when, walking through a subway tunnel to catch the Blue Line at O'Hare (and you know you can't get through the movie credits of any Chicago story without a shot of the El), I'd hear a saxophonist playing for tips. I'd walk by him with my practiced nonchalance, and his lonely, echoing sounds in the middle of all that concrete and motion made me feel like I was on the set of a play, a human drama about squalor, danger, and indifference. This, to me, was authenticity.

Chicago. There were songs, television shows, movies, and books about this place, and it seemed to me there could be no excuse for not having whatever you needed in a city so well known and likable it went by five or six nicknames.

When a familiar emptiness tried to creep up on me, I sprinted for a copy of the *Reader,* a fat weekly at the forefront of the town's possibility trade. Here was where you found the people, the jobs, the apartments, and the activities that could change the rest of your life, or at least the rest of your weekend. There were roughly five million ads in every issue, each a tiny beacon of hope in a sea of endless options.

I'd been in the city for several months when I saw, in the *Reader,* an ad for Sports Monster, a company that ran basketball leagues for adults. For sixty-five dollars, you got to play in six games plus a tournament with officials and score clocks, and you could go to league parties. There was a T-shirt, too.

And it hit me, sitting there with a highlighter in my hand, staring at so much possibility, that I wanted to play, bad. I didn't have a team put together, or a single acquaintance who would consider playing basketball in front of people. I myself hadn't played much at all since the days in the driveway. Sports Monster said that was no problem, and they signed me up as an independent on a coed team. They were very accommodating.

I forced my feet to move up the sidewalk to the gym that first Sunday we were scheduled to play. Inside, games were running one after another, and the bleachers were crowded. I looked around until I found some of my obvious teammates, three thirtyish single women congregating on the sidelines, each, like me, a long-ago high school player signed on as an independent. We introduced ourselves and chattered, saying lots to each other but avoiding the desperate-sounding articulation that Sports Monster would be a good way to meet men or at least lose a few pounds.

We found the guys on our team, a group of rogue hockey players from a Sports Monster league that had been canceled that year. Our team name, which had been chosen by Will, leader of the hockey guys, was Nothin' But Net. The name would prove to be appropriate only in an ironic sense.

We awkwardly readied ourselves to play. The buzzer sounded, the jump ball was tossed, and after a few trips up and down the court, it was clear the hockey guys understood that the general aim of basketball is to move the ball forward and keep the other team from it, and to get the ball in the hoop, preferably your own, but you could say many of the sport's finer points escaped them. The hockey guys might have caught an NBA game on television once, but they played the way you would expect hockey guys to play, and after a few Sundays, our only distinction other than remaining winless was having the most fouls.

One of the league's advertising partners was a sports bar that gave free pizza certificates to the winners every week. The teams that trounced us into the ground often gave us their certificates, saying they didn't have time for the sports bar. We'd always take the pizza. It seemed we were usually looking for things to do and free food.

Postgame, we women chatted about classes being taken, stints with the Peace Corps, or our impressive jobs. We were all good catches with no boyfriends in sight, the kind of straightforward, low-maintenance women that meddling mothers try and fail to convince their sons to date. The sad truth was, the majority of males—easily intoxicated by the delicate way an unfathomable woman might apply her lipstick—declined to ponder our Sweaty Betty hearts as we dove for balls and cut neutral figures in our baggy shorts and T-shirts.

The hockey guys navigated the social waters with a good number of adult cartoon references and debates over who was hotter, this movie star or that one. They didn't have significant others either, perhaps because, just as we women were neglecting our preening and subterfuge, their economic incentives remained underdeveloped. Dave, who had chronic trouble coming up with league fees, worked part-time in a sporting goods store and lived in his parents' basement. His chick magnet status was not enhanced by being a cruel brand of skinny assembling an extra-large Adam's apple, bad posture, and general wimpiness.

Even though Dave was our only player over six feet, the lane was, for him, foreign territory not to be entered without backup forces. He saw himself as a shooting guard, and he could be relied on to take it up just about every time he got the ball, like he wanted to get his money's worth, or rather the money's worth of whoever had floated his league fees that season.

Our standard offense was to come down court, leave the lane entirely empty, and pass the ball around the perimeter until it got to Dave, who would shoot and miss. If the shot took a wild bounce off the rim, we might luck into an offensive rebound and the chance to miss again, but usually Dave's attempts simply fell into the wide-open lane for the defense to catch like a bounce pass. Then Dave would hang back and cuss while the rest of the guys took off at full sprints to knock down the man with the ball before he could score. After the offense had been sufficiently subdued, my male teammates would thrust two victorious fists into the air and look over at the bench, anticipating cheers.

An infrequent variation happened when Amy, our best girl, posted up in the lane. Her athletic instincts sometimes got the better of her good sense, and she'd put her hands out and ask for the pass. We'd get the ball in to her, and she'd square around and shoot, undoubtedly feeling like her old high school self for a lovely, fleeting moment. But all the other teams actually had their *guys* playing in the lane, leaving the women on the wings like hood ornaments. Inevitably, a six-foot dude batted Amy's effort into the stands so suddenly and with such force that it was as if the ball, no longer willing to suffer the violations of our athletic fiasco, had hightailed it under a bleacher to hide.

As the ref hopped up into the stands to fish the ball out, the other team's bench hooted and hollered, shaming the blocker for rejecting a girl's shot like that. Things pretty much went as usual from there.

Another guy on our team, Matt, had the overbite, thick glasses, and sharp facial features of a born nerd. Throughout the season he systematically attempted to date all the women on the team, calling us on Friday evenings and asking could he pick us up in two hours to go to Navy Pier. He proposed the same outing to each of us, and we all said no.

Matt often tried to chat one of us up before a game. His chosen victim would bounce a ball around and take shots, and Matt would stand too close and hover. She'd dodge him, braying with nervous enthusiasm at his various inanities, then shooting the ball and running like hell to get her own rebound. Matt took these distracted niceties as green lights for his affection, trailing his bachelorette-of-the-day through timeouts, halftime, and donated pizza and beer. If only his defense had been so hard to shake.

The leader, Will, worked at his father's landscaping company and made self-deprecating jokes about "mowing yards for a living." I thought his work sounded pretty cool, myself. I admired that he could tell people what he did in a day without saying "implement" or "reorganize" or "going forward, our key takeaways are."

Over time we discovered there had been a brief, doomed engagement in Will's past, and the shadowy details of his broken heart gave him an air of maturity and a certain dark mystique, compared to Dave and Matt anyway.

Every team in the league had its own identity. One group was all attorneys and doctors and called itself Everyday People. The North Siders were a bunch of Polish Catholic brothers and sisters and cousins from the same family.

We didn't win a single game. A girl on our team who could shoot a little left Nothin' But Net to play with a more promising bunch of professionals who talked about the progress they were making on their MBAs. It was a better place to meet the right kind of people than our ad hoc ensemble of a not-knowing-anybody mess. I started calling the girl's new team the Corporate Clones, and Will laughed a little too hard when I said it.

One of the girls and I stayed on for the next season. The guys stayed, too, playing in both the basketball and hockey leagues.

Every Sunday they brutalized their bodies on the field before limping over to have their pride traumatized on the court.

We won our first game during the third season, accepting our pizza and beer coupons with pride. Maybe it's a little sad that, at this apex of achievement, my time with the Sports Monster league was coming to an end. I had started going to different parks to get in pickup games, an activity I was able to muster up the courage for thanks to Nothin' But Net, which had taught me, if nothing else, to look unflinchingly into the eyes of humiliation.

The more street ball I played, the more I wanted that old go-all-day freedom of the driveway. Sitting in my urban hovel apartment or working at my new job or making chitchat at dinner with multicultural men, my mind drifted to my high-tops, my ball, my bike, the court. A game was always out there, calling me into the street, and I answered, every chance I got.

Funny, what a convoluted route it can be to wanting what's home.

Nothin' But Net finished the season with a record of one and seven, and a new girl on the team threw a Christmas party for us. None of us were dating each other, or apparently anybody else, because we all came to the party alone.

The girl's new condo seemed especially warm that night, with its Christmas tree and coffee table full of dirty glasses and all its walls coated with fresh, hopeful paint. It was the sort of party you suffer through fifteen bad ones for, a gathering where everyone is just tipsy enough, and it's impossible to do anything other than act like you've got good sense.

It was getting late when I found myself sitting alone on the couch, relaxed and unworried about not mingling for the moment. Dave sat down and snuggled into the cushions beside me, and, at the feel of his bony hip against mine, I began to snicker. He hunched his rounded shoulders to lean in close to me and coo, "You and me, Melissa, we got chemistry."

It was nonsense, and he knew it, and I was charmed. My giggle was all that was needed to egg him on.

"Don't deny it now," he said, his voice hypnotic with goodwill and disregard for consequences. "You know it's true."

Will sat on the other side of me, saying nothing but jokingly focused on me as if he, too, had always thought I was all that. Matt stuck to his corner, watching and looking confused.

We held at bay for a few more minutes the frigid walks to our far-parked cars as we enjoyed being the hockey guys, the losingest team in Sports Monster history. Unlike Everyday People or the North Siders or the Corporate Clones, we'd earned the right to come together and laugh at ourselves. I barely noticed at the time how happy that felt, carried along as I was in the larger movement of always leaving.

At Eckhart Park, this court where I used to play in my neighborhood, there were three Latino guys I played with sometimes. The first time I saw them, one of the guys was wearing a T-shirt that said I LIKE MY HUSBAND, BUT I LOVE MY SNOWMOBILE.

He didn't speak English too well, and my theory was he bought the T-shirt at a thrift store because he liked the color, which was, actually, an appealing purple. Somebody must have told him what "husband" meant, because he had taken white shoe polish and marked out the word. You could still see what it said, but I guess the shoe polish effort let everyone know, *yo soy heterosexual.*

The guys were new to the game, and they played hard, running after loose balls and hustling for rebounds and playing good defense. The most experienced player, who was also the tallest and the best English speaker, was the one who'd asked me if I wanted to play. I'd been at the other end of the court shooting baskets, making furtive glances at them. It wasn't difficult for me to get noticed, being the only woman and the only white person on the court.

The way things worked was, I would shoot around, make a point to have them notice me noticing them, act slightly tough and a bit boyish, as if to say, "I got *skills.* I play all the time. I know what you're thinking, but what you better be thinking is, are *you* good enough to play with *me?*"

Eckhart was the kind of place I liked to find when I went out looking for a game. It usually wasn't too serious there, and every player filtered crazy differences in size, skill, or experience through his brain to come up with an approach to how hard he'd play, how hard he'd expect his teammates to play, how much he'd get in the lane, and how much trash he'd talk. It was the kind of place that might make room for a kid with Down syndrome, a guy with only one good hand, and people so hopelessly uncoordinated they could barely run, much less hit a jump shot. You'd see dunking studs there, too. There was a little bit of everything in the games I liked.

When a court was really competitive, that was okay, too. Sometimes I'd play, and sometimes I'd just walk on to go look for ragtag situations where everyone played hard but they let the guy with one good hand catch his pass and they let the kid with Down syndrome get his shot off.

I've always tried to look like I have some game when I'm dribbling around trying to get in, but I never say too many cocky things like "I got skills," or "Get that weak shit outta here," or "Not in my house, baby," or much of anything else, really. Words can get squirrelly sometimes, and I know I'm just an average type of player. I don't even wear that great of shoes or flashy sports clothes, because I never want what I'm wearing to be better than I am. I mean, I don't want to look like I don't know how good I'm not.

So I did my furtive checking-out routine, and when the tall, good-English-speaking guy asked me to play two-on-two, I did. My team won two games in a row. I played some more after that, with another group of guys. The teams kept melding and interchanging with new groups of people coming to play.

The sun baked the concrete, and there was a slightly sickening smell of sweetness and chocolate in the air from a nearby candy factory. An ice cream vendor came by from time to time, his bell tinkling pleasantly. Everyone on the court was speaking Spanish, and while Snowmobile and his crew were there, they interpreted for me if I gave them a look that asked what was happening.

After they left, the only words I could make out were *choc-oh-lah-tay*, seemingly directed at the only black kid on the court, and *niña*, me.

I stayed for hours, forcing my body to keep moving long after I was too tired to be there. My legs shook as I pedaled west up Chicago Avenue toward home. It was typical of my routine.

A few days later, I saw the Latino guys sitting on the grass and watching a serious five-on-five game. Snowmobile #1 wasn't there this time, and Snowmobile #2 and #3 were having trouble getting in. I sat down on the ground next to them.

We chatted for a while as the game moved up and down the court. They told me they were taking an English class four times a week, and they apologized because they couldn't speak English. I told them yes they could.

I had three semesters of Spanish in college, but I can barely speak a word of it. And I made As all three times, for God's sake. It's *hard* to learn another language. I kept wishing I could say things in Spanish to those guys and to all the Spanish-speaking people around my neighborhood.

I couldn't understand why the Snowmobiles weren't getting in the game. For me, being a woman, sometimes I just get the sense that a court is not exactly an equal opportunity situation, but it seemed like any guy should be able to play.

They said they weren't good enough. I told them yes they were.

A young black kid bounced his ball around on the side of the court, pacing, yelling at the players in the game, "I'm gonna kick y'all's tired asses when I get in there!"

Snowmobile #2 told me I could join them next weekend at this park they played at sometimes where there was always plenty of room. "They have sodas," he said.

Back in college, when I was taking those Spanish classes, I sometimes had dreams that I could really speak Spanish. In my dreams the words flew out in whole sentences with a perfect accent, and I didn't have to struggle or even think about it. Now that I was playing outside again, I was having that same kind of dream about basketball. I'm making every shot, flying toward the basket, never tired, no one can stop me.

Waking up from that dream on weekdays, I felt like a house dog chasing rabbits in her sleep, legs twitching.

I took this racquetball class one time. My partner was a slightly plump, likable girl with a blond, swingy ponytail, and what I remember most about her was how the instructor's face lit up when she came around. She and I played each other every class, and one time, after I'd won a few games in a row, she said to me, smiling and as nice as ever, "You should let me win sometimes."

She would have fit in well at the women's open gym I went to for a while. The players there stuck together like that, the athletic version of girls who don't go to public bathrooms by themselves.

The women's open gym met every Monday night at a Park District complex on Chicago's North Side. Most of us were professionals in our late twenties and early thirties, and white, with the exception of Tori, a black woman from the West Side who often made remarks about all the white faces. She seemed to like us and everything, but I noticed how often she pointed out that she was different.

The open gym had been started years earlier by a high-ranking Park District employee who was still a regular player. We were all supposed to contribute some money to keep the court reserved, but we never did, because we were in good with Jack, the guy who worked the front desk. Jack controlled that gym like a potbellied grizzly bear in tube socks and polyester coaching shorts. He liked us, or maybe he was just paranoid that, if he didn't kiss our asses, the high-ranking player would get him fired through some strange and twisted power she wielded from her office job at the Park District.

We weren't exactly "I got next" types. Instead of showing up and looking like we had game, we used Jack as our backup in a weekly coup over the kids who filled the gym until we got there. The minute the clock hit six Jack lumbered onto the court and roared at them to get out, abruptly ending all the kickball and chase going on as the shorties scattered to the nearest exits.

When we had too few women to play full-court, Jack still kicked the kids off the other end. It would've been easy for one of us to give him the nod that it was okay for them to stay, but nobody nodded. We couldn't let up like that, because control over the court depended on the mean-teacher authority we assumed when any kid considered sticking a toe across the out-of-bounds line between six and nine. It made me feel a little bad, grown women kicking kids off a court like that, but I wanted to play, so I came back week after week, wondering where the kids went on the night we had the gym but never taking a stand.

You had to be careful at the women's open gym, because a frown on someone's face or an elbow swinging for a rebound or a too-abrupt "Over here! I'm open!" was not acceptable to some factions. They didn't like it if you were too intense like that, which I was.

The women wouldn't call fouls, but they got mad if they thought you fouled and you didn't call it on yourself. That's just how they were. Of course, it was completely acceptable and well regarded when this one woman called official timeouts during every game to readjust a barrette or take off one of her five necklaces while everyone stood waiting. The girl shot two-handed from the center of her chest, and she traveled so much we finally quit calling it unless a game was at stake or it was just too obvious to ignore. Then we'd call the walk and she'd argue that it wasn't, even though she knew less about basketball than anyone. She never listened to anybody, and she never got much better. People could get by with that kind of thing there.

As bad a player as the traveling girl was, she did have a natural basketball player's body: tall and skinny, but strong. Her crazy-looking shots went in more often than they had a right to, and when she stuck her mile-long arms out on defense, she deflected shots like a windmill. She was pretty annoying, but sometimes she'd bring her two little boys, who were four and five, and they were so cute and happy and well behaved, sitting on the sidelines and cheering for their mom, that it made her seem okay.

Two of the women, one a decent enough player and the other not so much, would work on dribbling drills, the kind we used to do in high school, before everyone arrived at the gym. I was a little snobbish about the drills, I have to admit. I thought they weren't very street, and I'd shoot around by myself while the two women practiced dribbling between their legs.

Before we started playing one night, Tori, the black chick, and Melinda, the decent enough dribbler, got into a discussion about whether or not the large, fluffy-looking person we all saw as we were walking into the gym was a teenage boy or a woman in her twenties. Tori had just gotten there, and she changed into her basketball clothes standing on the sidelines in the gym. It was a little brazen, but people hadn't started arriving yet.

"It's a guy," Tori said, standing there in her sports bra.

"She has breasts," Melinda argued.

"Well, he's not wearing a bra then."

"So?"

John, an inexplicable and regular exception to the no-kids/no-men rule, was there. It was just the four of us because there was no air conditioning, and it was really too hot to play. We were the diehards.

John had a thin, very basketball-looking slump about him that reminded me of a poster a guy I used to date had hanging on his wall. The poster was called "Skins and Shirts," and it was a drawing of a bunch of black men going up for a rebound at the same time, stretched out all long-limbed and elegantly gangly toward the sky, everyone on both teams moving in what looked from a distance to be a synchronized unit, like a flock of geese making instinctual in-flight formations. John looked like those guys in that poster.

John was listening to the conversation about the androgynous employee, but, as usual, he wasn't saying much. He was a spooky kind of guy, with wide-open eyes that were a little crossed, and if a ball bounced off the rim toward him, he ducked and covered his head like he was being shot at. When you tried to talk to him, he answered with an abrupt nod or shake of his head, or one word at the most. I was kind of afraid of John when I first met him, but I figured out after a while that he was all right. Thinking back on it now, I guess he was a little afraid of us.

John was shooting around, looking like he was in his own world, but not really, and I said, "Hey, John, do you think that person working the front desk is a man or a woman?"

"Boy," he blurted, looking at me from the corner of one eye.

"This guy walked by me once," Melinda said, taking a shot. "It was really cold. I was bundled up and waiting for the bus, and he walked by and he goes, 'Hey, dude.' I told him, I said, 'Hey, I'm a woman.'"

Then Tori said she was in a car wreck once, and while she was waiting for the ambulance to arrive, she was laid out on the floor of a convenience store in layers of Chicago winter clothes. People kept coming up and looking over her and saying, "What's up with dude? What's up with dude?" She said she drifted in and out of consciousness saying, "Hey, I'm a woman."

We never did come to any conclusions about the person at the front desk.

Maybe it was that old, painful memory of being mistaken for a man that made Melinda especially sensitive to our gay invasion, made up of two openly lesbian players who were regulars for a while.

One of the gay hoopsters always wore a baby blue North Carolina mesh basketball set with a matching do-rag wrapped around her head all tight and smooth and tied in the back. The girl was pretty intimidating on the floor, and she was good, but she was mostly intimidating, with her authentic basketball garb and her swagger and her tendency to grab her crotch when she laughed and to give her teammates chest bumps when they did something good. She certainly had court presence.

She always told everybody it wasn't that serious, while she played her ass off. When she did something she was proud of, she'd break out in a current hip-hop dance move that most of us couldn't achieve even if you paid us.

Her girlfriend sat on the sidelines and watched, looking like somebody's mom in her regular jeans and glasses. She kept score for us, and she laughed a lot.

It was a real luxury to have someone keeping score, because it's hard to play and remember the score at the same time. We sure as hell needed lesbians to have a scorekeeper on hand. Nobody's *boy*friend would have sat on the sidelines and kept score. I never once saw a *boy*friend even come to watch. The girlfriend never was wrong on the score either. She always got it right, and everyone knew it and never argued with her. And she never acted bored or told her girlfriend to hurry up and get through playing either. They had a pretty good relationship, as far as I could tell.

One night not long after the invasion, Melinda and Tori and I were the first ones there again. As we shot around and waited for the others to arrive, Melinda said the two lesbian players touched her in inappropriate ways, and she didn't care if someone was gay, but why did they have to be so obvious about it?

That was crap, of course. Melinda cared all right. Those lesbians were just playing defense.

There was a television commercial airing around that time that showed a WNBA player talking about what she liked to buy on her credit card. "I'm very prissy," she would say, and the camera would go to another scene showing her playing street ball with a bunch of guys, screaming like a crazed warrior, "Put up or shut up!" as she drove the basket.

"I love to get my hair done, get manicures, pedicures, but my greatest weakness is shoes," she said, and then we were back to her discussing what she bought with her credit card as she walked through a mall in a trendy outfit.

The WNBA was just getting started then, and the commercials were hell-bent on proving that the league was full of nice, tall girls who did all the things nice girls are supposed to do. It made me wonder why women have to try so hard—why we have to declare a shoe obsession or slobber over chocolate or sit at the movies and pine at romantic comedies, why we always have to seem a little stupid or a little crazy—to qualify as socially acceptable females. The way some women talk with such pride about their greatest weakness sounds as fake as a politician sometimes: safe, pseudo-edgy personalities lifted directly from sitcoms and greeting cards.

Years later, an athletic shoe ad airing on WNBA commercial breaks showed a bunch of guy cheerleaders doing the exact same stripper moves their female counterparts do, but instead of looking sexy, they looked ridiculous. The camera showed the guys shaking their butts with scared, desperate-to-please looks on their faces, and then we saw a group of WNBA players huddled in a timeout, casually slouched and grinning, having an authentic time, ignoring the cheerleaders like athletes always do. The commercial seemed like an improvement, an evolution, from the credit card's pledge of allegiance to the shopping mall. The players didn't have to vow their dedication to manicures in order to be acceptable. They just had to play their game.

At the open gym or anywhere else, I wanted to win, but going for rebounds, screaming like a karate master, wringing wet with sweat, making faces I probably wouldn't want to see, it felt kind of weird. Sometimes it would occur to me, *Damn, I'm intense. I'm aggressive.* Not assertive—aggressive.

Tori said to me once, after one of my high, loud rebounds, "Girl, you're like a Reebok commercial. This is your world . . . you go." She could say stuff like that and manage not to sound like some advertisement. Maybe it was because she was black. Maybe it was because she meant it.

I didn't feel pretty and I didn't feel nice and I didn't feel prissy. I wasn't being distracted by candy or shiny trinkets or the perfection on my toenails. I did feel like myself, and it felt good.

The Wicker Park neighborhood was well into its urban pioneering days, but the park itself still reminded you of the area's relatively recent transformation. Hipsters threw Frisbees with their dogs a few hundred feet away from dozens of old-timers who had been killing time there since the days when Wicker Park really was a gritty urban neighborhood. In general, the old faction stuck to the Damen Street side, and the new people threw their Frisbees on the back end. There were savvy little independent kids running around all over.

Unlike the women's open gym, there were no guarantees at outdoor courts, no Jack guarding the door. Wicker Park was my Chicago, a place where I felt at home but didn't particularly belong.

Once, I saw a young couple with a large parrot. They were sitting on a blanket with a picnic basket, and a group of kids had gathered around them. I was bouncing a ball around on the court way across the park. From time to time the bird would raise its clipped wings and squawk and try to fly, and the kids would shriek and fall back, and then surge in to get a closer look. I was pretty amazed, thinking about the life of a city kid, seeing so much every day, and about how free-spirited or kind the couple might think they were for treating a crippled bird to a visit to the park.

A sign said WARNING YOU ARE IN A SAFETY ZONE. PENALTIES FOR SELLING DRUGS OR OTHER CRIMINAL ACTIVITY IN THIS PARK ARE SEVERELY INCREASED. I saw guys walk past each other making subtle handoffs, or drive up in separate cars, walk off together, then come back a few minutes later and take off again, going their separate ways. It was just what was happening, part of the bustle.

One day it was raining, and I got stuck sitting on my bike under an awning. When the weather cleared, I started shooting around. Three guys came over, and we played two-on-two. It was casual, no egos.

As it should've been, because they really sucked. They were fouling the hell out of each other, running around on the wet concrete, laughing and having a good time. One of them was wearing sandals, another was barefoot, and I think they were all three a little drunk. I was teamed with a guy named Vince, who had been the first to come over and shoot around with me.

There were four hoops crammed onto a small slab of concrete at Wicker Park. Most places, you play half-court unless you have at least eight, but here, games went to full-court at three-on-three because the courts were so short.

A dirt field beside the basketball courts was used for sixteen-inch softball, which I'd never seen until I moved to Chicago. I guess it's popular in the city because you don't need much room to play it. You can't hit that big-ass ball very far.

The three sucky-player guys and I played goofy full-court two-on-two, and on one particularly good play Vince stuck both hands behind his back, palms up, while he ran backwards down the court, for me to slap him ten. It was stupid, but he knew it was stupid. I like that in a person.

Vince wrote his phone number on my arm with a felt-tip pen after we finished playing. I wrote the number down somewhere when I got home, but later on I couldn't find what I did with it.

One day, I was sitting on my bike at Wicker Park, scanning the court, when I heard someone talking to me from the general direction of the Damen Street side.

"What's up, kittycat?"

This old park dude was looking at me, grinning.

"What's up, kittycat, you gonna shoot some hoops you gonna play me some one-on-one can you dunk it?"

I almost turned around and rode off, because I knew this guy was gonna stick to me the whole time I was there, but there was an empty hoop and I felt irritated about having to leave a court because of this old park dude, especially after I'd ridden all the way over there on my bike.

The guy I mentioned earlier, the one with the "Skins and Shirts" poster, always said I should stay away from unsavory elements. He thought I was reckless. He wouldn't ride the El, and he never gave money to homeless people on the street. But he volunteered at shelters around the holidays and was on the boards of several charitable organizations.

Park Dude went walking off somewhere, so I shot for a while, and then he came back and started shooting around with me.

There's a certain etiquette when people shoot around. Sometimes someone just comes up and starts getting your rebounds, sort of deferring until you pass the ball to him and trot to the hoop to get his rebounds. Or sometimes people come up to you if you're shooting and just say, "Can I shoot around?" and you say sure.

Usually, when two people shoot around, one person shoots from the outside and the other stands under the hoop and rebounds until the shooter misses. Then the shooter comes in for a lay-up and starts rebounding for the other person. That's pretty customary.

Park Dude wasn't so great to shoot around with. He kept throwing the ball back to me too hard, or slinging it clear over my head or off to the side so that I had to jump or make a quick move to catch it or else it would get past me. Every once in a while the ball *did* get past me, and I would have to run after it, practically doing back flips to catch it before it flew onto another court or rolled into the middle of a softball game.

If I were male, younger, urban, I would have said something like, "Man, would you *watch* that shit? What's the matter with you? *Damn.*" But I'm not.

I have to admit, though, Park Dude could really shoot a hook shot. He barely even looked at the goal but just threw it in the general direction and made it, nothing but net. It was a "patented shot," something a lot of older guys develop to compensate for their diminished games.

After a while, I found myself in a game with Park Dude and some kids. A little girl asked me how old I was. She nearly fell over when I told her I was thirty.

"How old are you?" I asked her.

"Ten," she told me.

Park Dude ran after his own rebound after missing wildly. The little girl looked after him, crinkling her face.

"He's weird," the girl said. "He smells like beer."

He was, and he did, but as far as I could tell, there was nothing wrong with his hearing. Park Dude laughed at something. He said it was getting hot, and he took his shirt off. There was a long, vertical scar running down his rib cage and stomach.

That's when I began to worry. I started to think about what happens to a harmless park dude's brain when he's treated like dirt by arrogant little white girls. And then I actually did begin to feel like I was reckless, understanding for real that I was the one who had brought Park Dude and the little girl together. She would have never come over had she not seen me there, and I didn't know how safe it was for me, much less for her.

We played for a while longer, and the little girl relentlessly dissed everyone, including the two boys she'd come with. I couldn't tell whether her caustic attitude was genuine bad-ass or plain old fear, and I didn't know if it would get her in trouble or help her by making her seem tough. Park Dude laughed and seemed to approve. He kept turning his attention on her, as if he wanted her energy directed at him, no matter how disdainful she was. He seemed to be thinking, *You go, girl,* but I couldn't really tell for sure. I just felt sort of uneasy and responsible.

After the game, I said I had to go. But I hung around a minute or two on my bike, watching the court to make sure everyone had scattered before I rode home.

Some days, my natural foods job was beyond tiresome. My boss was a balding man who was shorter than I was and kept his ring of hair styled into a scrawny ponytail. It was my responsibility to help him get contracts together, which wouldn't have been too difficult except that it was near impossible to keep him focused. I always had to ha-ha it up for about a half hour while I waited for the moment when I could bring up the work we had to do in a way that wouldn't be a big downer for him. He ran the company with his wife, who was no picnic either, the way she came up behind her employees and gave us shoulder massages as we tried to keep typing at our keyboards. Personally, I didn't find that relaxing.

The structure of most weekdays was to hit the snooze alarm fifty times, muddle through eight hours, leave the office at 5:01, go home and change into some basketball clothes, and go looking for a game. It was on such a day that I ended up at Wicker Park, shooting around with a little kid, another little kid, and his toddler brother, killing time before a game developed.

I kept grinning at the toddler, because he was cute, but his brother didn't grin; he included him. He expected the child to play, but he wasn't too rough on him. The toddler just ran all over the court with his arms wrapped around the ball, grinning.

A commotion broke out on the other court, and everyone got still, stopping what they were doing to watch.

"Why you testin' me, nigga? . . . Why don't you test summa these other niggas!?" one of the kids was saying to a shorter kid, pushing him, in his face, itching to fight.

Two middle-aged guys were standing off to the side of the court. They were Park District employees. I could tell because they were wearing those plastic ID holders on their shirts, standing around with their arms crossed and surveying everything, talking to each other.

Everyone watched the escalating problem. After a boy got in the middle of the two fighters, one of the Park District guys walked over and said something.

"Gentlemen, gentlemen," the Park District employee kept saying. "Let's just play ball. Gentlemen." But those two kids didn't care about some middle-aged white guy with a potbelly and an ID tag. They just kept on.

"Man, if you ever touch my shit again, I'll kill you! Come on, nigga, swing! Do it!"

The tall kid stalked off, daring the other kid to follow and fight him. The older brother on my court looked over at the toddler and said gently, "Boo, wanna go see a fight?" Boo just laughed, running around in his stiff-legged toddler way, holding on to the ball.

After a while, an older guy asked me would I like to play with him and some other people. I said sure. The guy who'd asked me to play was the only adult among teens, and he played like it mattered. The kids were kind of laughing at him until we started kicking their butts. The older guy refused to scale down his intensity, saying to the scoffing teens, "You know I play hard." The teens got into it in spite of themselves, and we could never remember the score. That's how it is when the game is really good, like when you're having fun on your vacation and you don't remember to get out your camera and take a picture.

The morning's snooze-alarm abuse seemed like it was from someone else's life. I was on, lost in what I was doing, only erring a few times when I misjudged how fast those teens were and how high they could jump now that they were breaking a sweat. I'm not that great of a shooter, but that evening, as we began to feel the urgency of making one more trip down the court before it got too dark to play, I was hitting everything. The guys kept yelling at each other, looking for someone to blame every time I made a shot, yelling "Who's guarding that girl!" and calling me Little Larry Bird.

We all have our moments.

I'd get up on Saturday mornings knowing my apartment needed to be cleaned or something, but then I'd find myself in my car, cruising for a game. I'd start shooting around, tell myself I was only going to stay for a few games, but more often than not it was close to dinner time before I went home.

One morning I was at Wicker Park, bouncing a ball around casually and taking a few shots while I waited for people to wander up. A boy burst out of a nearby building and came running towards me.

"Hey! You wanna play me one-on-one?!"

We'd played on the same court a few times. I said, "Yeah, let's go," but before we could get started, the boy had to make time for some Wicker Park child care.

"Rolando!" a woman shouted from an ancient Cadillac idling in the street, causing him to stop everything and sprint to the car for instructions about when to come home. Then he raced back over as fast as he'd left, apparently cleared for some more time at the park. The Cadillac roared off.

"Come on! Let's go!"

He was practically yelling, he was so excited.

We shot around for a minute on the empty court.

"Where is everybody?" I asked him.

"My homeys just went to the store," he told me.

So I played him a game of one-on-one. He was only about ten years old, and I was two feet taller than he was, so of course I didn't guard him very hard.

His three homeys rode up on two bicycles. The Gap could only wish to get at the urban slouch of these kids' baggy T-shirts and shorts as they sat on two-thirds enough bicycle, watching Rolando and me play. One kid stayed balanced on the handlebars, confident as a cat.

They kept saying, "Yeah, she goin' to the WNBA next week. She got a right, she got a left, she got a shot, she got some D. . . "

They were just messing with me, being friendly because Rolando was.

Rolando kept teasing me, too, pretending he was shoving me around and laughing and shouting and showing off, saying stuff like "All right, it's on now," and "You know I'm mad now." I was kidding him back, saying, "Thanks for the warning, Rolando."

I liked that kid. I told him he was playing well, and he said, just a little more quiet and serious now, "Some people say I got game."

I tried to tell Rolando something my dad used to tell me about how, when you're playing defense, you need to look at someone's belly. How you don't look at their face, because they can fake you out with their face and eyes, but they can't fake you out with their belly. He looked like he knew about the belly already, but he seemed to like it that I was telling him something.

He said his coach always told him to keep his eyes on their bootie.

"That'll work," I said.

After a while, a group of teenage guys started playing a game of twenty-one on the other court. I hate that game sometimes because it's so heavily rebound-oriented. I love to get rebounds, but when it's all guys who are bigger than me, I do better passing and playing defense and shooting from the outside than I do driving the basket and getting rebounds.

"Rolando," I said, "do you think those guys would let me play with them?"

"I don't think so," he said. "They're kind of rough."

More and more of Rolando's friends started arriving, getting their own vibe going. The courts were filling up, and I couldn't find a place on either side. I shot around a little longer, but those older guys never asked me to play or even made eye contact with me, even though I knew they saw me wanting to get in the game.

I went back home to face my dirty dishes, thinking how those sonsofbitches made me sick. They didn't know if I could play or not.

The next time I played with Rolando, he was being guarded by a girl about his age and size. Between plays, the girl busted the standard "this sister's seen it all and ain't takin' no shit off yo' punk ass" move, that combination hand-head motion that, joined with some colorful profanity and threats of hitting someone with a chair or a shoe, never fails to thrill a Jerry Springer audience. On a ten-year-old, the attitude was a little ill-fitting, like she was wearing her mother's high heels.

Rolando was being his usual gregarious self. I started playing with him and the girl and some other kids, hoping a ragtag group of adults looking for exercise would begin to form.

Some people play with quiet intensity. Not Rolando. He never quit talking, and he was always having an elaborate fit over a good play somebody made, or yelling for everyone to throw him the ball all the time. He was often offended if he was left out on a fast break. Once, as his teammates trotted back down court after making a lay-up, he stood on the defensive end yelling, "Oh yeah, now, see, ya'll just forgot all about poor Rolando, didn't you?"

His teammates looked at him like he was crazy, which he was, a little. He'd been nowhere near the play.

Our game ended, and Miss Seen It All, she homed right in on

good-humored Rolando, using him to make an impression on the group, telling us exactly how things were gonna be.

"I can play," she said, looking at Rolando, "and I play to win, so don't you even be tellin' me I can't get in this game, cause I'm tellin' you right now, I'm the best."

Rolando looked at her like he didn't know quite what to say. No one was trying to keep her out.

Then, with one quick move, the girl threw the ball on the ground behind her and started chasing Rolando around, and he was laughing, but he didn't look exactly unafraid, and I noticed he managed to stay out of arm's reach of her. I could see the whites of his eyes as he looked back over his shoulder, trying to determine if he was playing or fighting.

She'd made her point, and we began to play. She actually did have a little game, too. After a while, she left, leaving Rolando, me, and a few others.

He came over to me, quiet for once, his head bent over the basketball he was bouncing two-handed and hard, like he was a little put out.

"That girl, she sure talks a lot," he said.

I suggested she seemed to have no lack of confidence.

"Yeah, too much confidence."

"Whaddya call that?" I asked.

"Anger," Rolando said without hesitation.

My friend Laurie back in Arkansas used to tell me how she couldn't go to church without about three guys asking her out. It was the biggest pickup situation you ever saw, evidently, because everyone there had this big dream of meeting somebody at church. She would joke that all the single people at her church were "datin' for Jesus!"

Well, the same thing can happen with basketball. I met this guy. Let's call him Peter. I saw him one day, looking at me all intense from the other end of the court. He made sure he got in the game I was in, and then he hung around afterwards and asked if I wanted to go have a drink later. I said I did. He was good-looking and a pretty good player, too.

Some guys never get past how they met you. For instance, I met a guy at a dog party once. It was a dog party because it was a party that everyone brought their dogs to, and it was supposed to help you mingle and meet other dog owners. It was pretty awkward, trying to make a good impression while struggling to keep the dogs from fighting or inappropriately sniffing the other partygoers, but everyone was doing the best they could.

I went to the dog party with this girl I worked with who kind of talked me into it. Neither of us actually had a dog, so we took the natural foods office dog, Penny. We knew Penny pretty well because it was everyone's job to baby-sit her while we worked.

The bosses fed Penny a supplement called Green Strength, which was made from grass, so the dog threw up a lot. Penny's green puke really stained the carpet, so when she started heaving by the door, we'd jump up from our chairs and try to hustle her outside. It wasn't so great of a job, as I've previously implied.

The coworker borrowed a dog to go to the party, that's how frantic she was to go. I've found that single women in their thirties are always latching on to each other to go do cute stuff like that. They're not exactly friends or anything, but they need someone to go do these supposedly man-meeting things with. If you say no, you feel guilty, because you know they want to go so bad, and they won't go by themselves. It's pretty depressing.

So at the dog party, this guy, Ed, decided he liked me. And he did everything right. He asked me out for a polite date, he introduced me to his friends, always asked me for the next date before he left. He was sweatin' me, as they say.

But there was no connection, really. I couldn't help thinking that the only reason he wanted to go out with me—I mean, the reason it was me and not somebody else—was that he could just imagine telling everybody how we met at a dog party when I didn't even have a dog. Very *That Girl.*

People don't want to say they met in a bar or on matchmaker.com. There's always got to be some damn cute story or you don't have a chance.

So the guy from the court, Peter, was all over me because he'd met me the way he envisioned meeting *the* woman—on the basketball court. That's what he said: "I always wanted to meet a woman on the basketball court."

There have been times when I've gone months without a date, but I must have had pheromones then, because there was this guy at the Park District gym who kept asking me out, too. He was part of a coed group I played with on Wednesday nights for a while, and he made me mad when he started flirting and trying to be all charming with me, because I'd already heard that stupid dumb-ass say he had a girlfriend. Oh, and guess what: the girlfriend lived in another city. Lucky me!

The thing about some people is, they'll ruin every last thing you like if you let them. So you can't let them. I dodged the guy with the girlfriend, but Peter and I went out for a few weeks. We rode our bikes to the lake, played basketball, sat on park benches kissing. All very romantic.

He was funny, but he wasn't the kind of funny where he knew he was funny. One time we were going to ride bikes, and I rode by his house to meet him. He came out of the house carrying a bottle of wine, some plastic cups, a corkscrew, and two bed sheets to sit on. He was carrying all of it in a white plastic garbage bag. That stuff can be kind of endearing, but only if the guy is good-looking.

When he kissed me, he was always pulling the back of my hair. I had short hair, and his hand slipped when he tried to pull, and I had a hunch that he was wishing I had longer hair so he could really grab on and give it a good yank. I wanted to say hey, what the hellareya doin', but I didn't.

One night he asked me over to his house to watch the Bears game. I was a little late getting there, and when he answered his door, he looked at me kind of sternly and said, "You're late." You could tell he didn't appreciate it.

Peter had a beer in his hand, and there were two joints sitting on the kitchen counter. He was talking a mile a minute. In fact, I was starting to notice that Peter didn't let you get a word in edgewise. And if he didn't think you were listening well enough, he would get right in your face and talk louder.

So we sat down to watch the game, and he lit up one of the joints. For some reason, I smoked a little. I used to smoke in college, but I hadn't in a long time. I'd quit because I used to get too paranoid on it. I'm kind of self-conscious generally, and pot just makes it worse.

So I smoked some, and Peter smoked a lot, and boy, did I get messed up. I found myself wondering whether Peter was really stupid, or just pretended to be as a joke. And I hadn't really noticed that trait before. I mean, he wasn't by any means the smartest guy I'd ever run into, but I just thought he was really physical, that he related to the world in a physical way. But now that I was high, there was no getting around the fact that he wasn't the sharpest stick in the bunch.

One of my problems has always been that if I think a guy is good-looking, and if he entertains me at all, and if he seems to like me, I can make excuses for him and overlook some pretty bad behavior. A lot of women do that. Decent men without girlfriends must really get sickened by it. I know I would.

So I was sitting in this chair, really stoned, trying to sit up straight, when Peter sat down beside me in the chair, put his arm around me, and started absentmindedly digging his fingers into my arm, hard. It seemed compulsive. It was like he couldn't help himself, it felt so good to him. And then, and this is really embarrassing, Peter got up and started gyrating around like a Chippendale dancer, saying, "So, what should I do? . . . Do you want me to dance for you?" I just kept hoping he meant to be cheesy and make me laugh. But I didn't laugh, because I was afraid he was serious.

To make things worse, I was having a lot of trouble concentrating because, in addition to trying to sit up straight, I was worried about my face. I didn't want anyone to see my facial expressions, because I felt like I had no control over my face.

All I could think of to say was, "Man, I'm stoned."

All of a sudden, Peter picked me up and carried me toward an open window. I never like it when guys physically pick you up. I know it's supposed to be romantic, but I just think it's embarrassing. It's too dramatic unless they're going to laugh and maybe act like you're so heavy they're going to throw their back out or something.

Then I started to worry that Peter might just chuck me out the window if he felt like it. I really did. I squirmed to get down without saying why, and then Peter assured me he wouldn't throw me out no window.

It seemed to me that the idea of throwing someone off a second story for no particular reason should have been so preposterous that it wouldn't have occurred to him, and that's when I started getting really scared. Peter's face looked brutish, and when he moved anywhere near me, it felt like he was trying to dominate me physically, not just get close. I managed to wriggle free of his King Kong–like grasp, and he tried to pick me up on his back, like we were going to play piggyback. Things were making no sense whatsoever.

His movements were slow and, I don't know, just slow, like a dumb animal's. I got the distinct impression he wanted to hurt me. That even if I had sex with him willingly he would still want to hurt me.

Peter was lumbering around saying, "Why're you so afraid of me? Try to have a little confidence why don'tcha . . . I know I can make you feel good," and other creepy stuff like that. I got the hell *out* of there, brushing past him, down the stairs, walking at a near trot to my car, sitting down in the driver's seat and locking the doors, fast. It was only a few minutes' drive to my house, but it took longer since I got lost three times trying to get there, thinking the whole time that I would truly go mad if I had to maneuver that car one more inch.

But like I said, I quit smoking pot because it makes me paranoid. And what did I expect, anyway, letting some only-cute guy into my game like that? Nothing good could have come of it.

· · ·

These three girls I'd seen before at Wicker Park came running over saying, "There's that girl again!"

They looked like the female version of the Fat Albert gang. I asked them if they wanted to shoot around, and the youngest one, who had about twenty-five different-colored barrettes in her hair and jeans at least three sizes too big, took the ball.

"I can't do it," she'd say every time she missed a shot.

"Yes you can, you just need to practice some. Nobody makes it every time."

"Why aren't you shootin'?" she asked me.

"I'm all right. Go ahead."

I've never seen any boy worry about if he was keeping you from playing.

One girl wouldn't play at all. We tried to play two-on-two, but she just wouldn't participate. She kept saying she didn't know how, and she couldn't make it, and all that stuff. She stood out on the court, though, right in the middle of everything. We'd pass her the ball, and she'd move out of the way and let it go past her.

The youngest one's younger brother came up and tried to play. He was running all over the court, never dribbling, a big grin on his face, saying, "Almost!" every time he shot and missed.

The girls didn't play very long, but they didn't leave either. They hung around the edge of the court, watching. You could see them kind of whispering together and looking at different boys.

"Where's you girls' boyfriends?" I asked them, just to see what they'd say.

"Twanisha got her a man," the little one said, pointing to the girl who wouldn't play.

"Where's Twanisha's boyfriend?"

"He over there with his boys."

"That why you won't play basketball, Twanisha?"

She shrugged her shoulders in reply.

They were doing it already, waiting around for something to happen. I wanted to give Twanisha a little shake and say, "Listen here, young lady, you're gonna spend your life falling for arrogant men and sitting around a dirty apartment waiting on the phone to ring if you don't start taking an interest in some things!"

If I had a daughter, she'd have to learn how to be smart and daring. I don't know how I'd teach her, because I don't even really know how myself, but somehow she'd have to know early on that it's okay to miss some shots, that you can't let other people always do your shooting for you.

I started playing with some adults, so I told a bunch of adolescent boys who had walked up they could play with my ball if they took care of it. It didn't take them long to get a big game going.

One of the kids defected to play with us. His name was Leon, and he was on my team. He was a foot shorter than the adults, but he could play. He was smart and serious about it. A kid on the other court was mad at Leon for his disloyalty. He was screaming, "Oh yeah, I see how it is! You wanna play over there with them. Man, I *hate* people like you!"

He was joined by a fellow glaring malcontent who ran up and said, "Can I play?" really sarcastic to us. There was tension, confused and racial, because most of the adults were white and all of the kids were black, but we were really segregated on the basis of age and size, not color. The two kids couldn't see this, or didn't want to.

Once our ball flew over onto their court, and the loud kid shot it into their hoop like he thought it was their ball from their game, or I should say, my ball. He looked over at us and said, all mock-innocent, "Oh, is that your ball?"

Leon wouldn't even look at them, and we got our ball back and kept playing. I kept glancing over at the other side to make sure my ball was there, but as our game was ending I looked up to find all the kids, and my ball, gone.

I asked Leon, "Hey, do you know those kids who were over there?"

"Which ones?"

"Those ones who were playing with my ball over there."

"Your ball? What's it look like?"

"Orange. Rubber."

"Man, I think they took off with it," Leon said, looking like he was trying to keep from laughing.

Lewis, another kid about Leon's size who was playing with us, said, "There they are. Hey, Thomas, you got that girl's ball?!"

There was the group, standing in the middle of a larger crowd about a hundred yards away. And there was my ball. I admired Lewis for taking a stand, and I wondered if Leon had known where the ball was.

"Come on, man, you got that girl's ball!" Lewis yelled. "Bring it back! Bring it back *now!*"

Thomas slung the ball across the playground at us, and I played a few more games, shaking off the heaviness of half-alive girls and boys who try to steal your shit just because you loaned it to them.

But then there was David, a five-year-old capable of redeeming the entire planet. He came to Wicker Park on Saturdays with his mom, who coached a bunch of girls in the gym.

I was matched up with David's mom in a pickup game once. It can be uncomfortable when two women who are used to playing with guys are put on each other. It draws a lot of sudden attention, two novelties taking each other on like that, and it makes me a little less intense. I still play hard, but it's awkward, wanting to win while feeling a loyalty to my sister-girl on the other team.

David's mom was an overall better player than I was, but I was faster and got my share of shots in. She was talking trash, having fun, treating me like any worthy adversary. As usual, I didn't really talk trash, and pretty soon she stopped, too.

After the game was over, I shot around, and David came over to talk to me.

"Where's your friend?" he asked me.

"What friend?"

"Your friend. She wears black shoes, too."

David thought he remembered me from somewhere, I guess. So I told him I didn't know who he meant and asked was he sure it was me he had seen before, and he said yes he was sure.

I asked him how old he was, and he said five.

"I play with my mama."

"You do? Was she the one who was playing with me a little earlier? She's pretty good."

She came over to shoot around with us.

"She made me in her stomach," David informed me. I said really, how 'bout that.

He whispered something to his mom. "Well, she's pretty good, too," his mom said.

A few months later I was playing two-on-two, and I saw David's mom again. She gave me a friendly wave and told the four of us who were playing that we could come inside the gym if we wanted to. After my outside game, I went in, and David came running over to me, shouting, "Hi, Melissa!"

I talked to him for a while and said it looked like his front teeth were growing back from the last time I saw him and asked him what he had been doing. Then he ran around all over the gym with kids his age while his mom and I and a bunch of teens played.

In the middle of the game, David came over and stood on the sidelines, yelling.

"Maaama! . . . Maaama! . . . *Maaaaaaama!*"

His mom, the point guard, picked up her dribble.

"What?!"

David hesitated, caught off guard by her attention.

"Do you want me?" he asked, looking at her expectantly.

"Do I *want* you?" she asked, her eyebrows raised, ball on her hip, like she couldn't believe what she was hearing.

David just kept looking at her, smiling, his eyes wide open, waiting.

"Yes," the mom said, "I want you, but not right this minute."

Satisfied, David continued with his running around, and we went on with our game.

The day after I heard about another women's open gym at the New City Y in Lincoln Park, I was filling out my paperwork, half-listening to the person behind the desk telling me all about the Y's many features I'd never use. Now I had a sure bet on Tuesday and Thursday nights, in addition to Mondays at the Park District gym. Life was good.

The Y was a blue brick building surrounded by huge upscale grocery stores and home decor shops on nearby North Avenue and housing projects across the street. The players there were a combination of good-job-having women and a bunch of girls from the untransitioned part of the neighborhood, and I liked the mix.

From six to seven, the floor was ours, and a perpetual group of adolescent boys would give up the court because, as they said with no resentment, "It's woman time." The boys would watch us make teams, hoping we wouldn't have enough players and would let some of them play. Sometimes that happened, but usually we had more than ten.

Kicking those kids off the court felt different than it had at the Park District gym. It was only for an hour, so the boys waited around instead of heading for the street, and the teenage girls who played with us knew the boys. It felt like we were taking turns, not invading something.

The players were friendly but direct at the Y, and if someone got mad at someone else or thought she fouled, or if she just didn't like the way someone was playing, she would say it right then and there and get it over with. It wasn't pissy like the Park District gym, but it was chaotic and nearly impossible to get a game organized, and that could be a pain when you wanted everyone to just shut up and play.

Sometimes I would swear a little bit if I did something really bad on the court. I'd try not to, because there was a big-ass sign on the wall that said NO HATS, NO DUNKING, NO CURSING, and because, since I was playing with kids, I thought I should set a good example and everything.

But sometimes it just came out. I said shit one time when I missed a lay-up, and a short, chubby teenager who was guarding me giggled for about ten minutes. Later, when we were down on the other end of the court, I really guarded her hard just to be silly, and we both laughed at me.

This other girl, Tina, was the chubby girl's best friend. Tina always wanted to play me one-on-one. She'd come running over as soon as she saw me, and if I missed a night, she'd want to know where I'd been.

Thoughts of Tina had a way of staying with me. I'd been meaning to "get involved" for some time, entertaining some pretty feel-good daydreams about mentoring, imagining myself taking my charge to the library or throwing a Frisbee with her in the park. After years of my good influence, my mentoree would go to college, where she would major in English literature or journalism and send me witty and incisive letters from her dormitory.

But when I thought about really getting involved, I couldn't see myself getting past the point of being introduced to my mentoree. I always imagined sitting across the table from a kid more jaded than precocious and being instructed to, okay now, mentor, and the at-risk youth would just look at me like she knew I was about to say something lame. I was too worried that I wouldn't think of something not lame to say, and my volunteer efforts never made it past the picking-up-pamphlets phase.

Tina was a little tomboy hotdog, fourteen years old or so, tall for her age and skinny with her hair always styled into two afro puffs. She had a habit of shooting the ball from about three feet in from half-court, missing the entire basket as often as not, with all her teammates yelling at her and groaning every time she took one of her hopeless shots. But she didn't care what anybody said. She just laughed this crazy hooting laugh she had and went on with what she was doing.

She was a good player, though, when she wasn't acting like a lunatic.

Tina lived in the projects with her mom, her mom's boyfriend, and three half-brothers and -sisters. "We all got different daddies," she told me once.

She knew the stereotypes, and knew she was one. She had a pretty good idea what people expected of her, and she generally met those expectations.

Tina often worried aloud about her brothers and sisters, especially one sister who was overweight. "I don't know whether she belongs on Jenny Jones or Jenny Craig!" Tina would shout, then fall out laughing with her hoots and howls.

Tina would follow me out to my car after our games, talking fast so the conversation couldn't end, and eventually, not wanting to blow her off, I'd sometimes give her a ride home, even though she lived so close she could have just as easily walked.

Before or after our main game, Tina and I would take on two boys her age. Sometimes she'd play serious, and sometimes when she was in one of her three-point moods, I'd try to steal the ball from her when she was on my own team, just as a joke.

One day, walking out of the building at the end of the night, she asked me if I'd show her how to drive. She told me she had her permit and it was legal for her to drive with an adult. Later, when I told someone about teaching Tina to drive, he told me she was probably lying about the permit. Maybe she was; I didn't really think about it at the time. I'm not very smart about knowing when not to believe people sometimes.

I drove us up North Avenue to the Bed Bath & Beyond parking lot, and I let her get behind the wheel of my Honda, which had a stick shift. She killed it three times trying to get it started, but then she got going, driving slowly around and around, with me regretting choosing a parking lot with actual parked cars in it. I was terrified, screaming, "*Stop, stop, stop, Tina, stop!*" and using my imaginary passenger's side brake.

Then I calmed down and told her she was doing great, that I definitely wasn't yelling at her; I was just nervous, that's all.

After about twenty minutes, we stopped the lesson and got out to change seats.

"Now that was some good drivin' there," she said.

"Yep, it sure was. You're a natural."

Another time, Tina asked me if I'd take her shopping for clothes at some stores north of the Y on Milwaukee. I knew that area, because it was near my apartment. The streets were crammed with wig shops, tiny rooms selling nothing but watches, and stores filled floor to ceiling with racks of pimp and fly girl clothes all wrapped in individual plastic bags.

I had once bought a bright yellow fiberfill-stuffed jacket at one of three athletic apparel stores on Chicago Avenue, a block from my apartment. I bought the jacket because I'd been wearing my dress coat—a long black thing with faux fur collar and cuffs—to the gym, with my white high-top cross trainers sticking out the bottom. I knew I looked like an idiot, but the dress coat was the warmest thing I had.

The store where I bought my jacket had an ironing board and seam ripper station, and as you checked out, someone asked if you wanted them to remove the knockoff logos that adorned 80 percent of your purchase's surface area. I had them take mine off.

I drove Tina up Milwaukee, but even though it was only a little after seven o'clock, every store up and down the street had its iron bars locked across the windows for the night. We tried to figure out where to go instead. There was nowhere to shop in the Y neighborhood, unless you liked expensive groceries or home improvement projects. The only clothing store over there that I knew about was a hiking place full of backpacks and eighty-dollar khaki shorts. And there was a Gap, too, but Tina wasn't really a Gap girl. She suggested we go to the Kmart on Ashland, where, after browsing in the young men's clothing section and finding nothing, she bought deodorant, a toy for one of her sisters, and a big poster with a poem on it titled "Follow Your Dreams."

I found myself talking to people about Tina sometimes. One friend told me I should be taking her to museums, not driving her around an empty parking lot. Another told me I better watch what I was doing, that I didn't know this little city kid, who was more than likely a lot savvier than I was. And he said I better never give her anything, either. That's what they told him in his mentoring program, never to give them anything.

One night at the Y Tina picked up her dribble to tell us she was afraid she was pregnant. She blurted it out, and no one really knew how to react to her. We just kept playing, Tina too, but she would get really mad and throw the ball against the wall or just give up and stay on her team's end of the court while everyone else got back on defense and yelled at her.

Tina followed me out to the car that night and told me again about being afraid she was pregnant, and I said, "Tina, what in the world are you talking about?"

That's when she told me this story.

"Well," Tina said, "last week, my stepdaddy and I got into it. We got into it real bad, and he was whippin' me like crazy, and I just couldn't take it no more. So I left the house and started walkin'."

"Okay . . ."

"I was just walkin' around, and it was gettin' later, and this older guy that I know from the neighborhood came up and started talkin' to me, and I didn't have nothin' to do, so I was talkin' to him in his car, and then he told me he'd give me a ride to this restaurant and we'd get somethin' to eat."

Tina paused, squinting off into the distance.

"Well, we didn't go to no restaurant. He took me down an alley, and I wondered what he was doing that for, but I didn't say nothin', and then . . . well, you know what he did was, he raped me, and that's why I'm afraid I might be pregnant."

"Oh my God, Tina," I guess I might have said. "Did you tell your mom? Did you tell your social worker?" (She'd mentioned the social worker several times, offhandedly, like the different daddies.)

"Yeah, I told my mom, and she took me to the doctor. But you know what? That man, that man in the car, he's got two kids, and he's married. That's what I couldn't believe."

Tina's mom had taken her to the emergency room after she'd made it home that night. She'd been tested for HIV and everything else, and the results were to come in the following week. I'm not sure why she didn't have the pregnancy results immediately. Maybe she did. Maybe she didn't believe or understand them. Maybe she could think of no better way to broach the subject than just shouting it out from midcourt.

"We were in that waitin' room for six hours," Tina said, "and then we went to see the doctor. And you know what she did? She took her hand . . . her *human* hand . . ."

Tina didn't finish her sentence. She just hooted, despite it all. We talked by my car for a long while.

"Tell me about that woman takin' your purse," she said.

"About when I was mugged? I told you about that three times already."

"I know, tell me again."

I paused, making it seem like Tina was having to drag it out of me.

"Hmmm. Okay. Well, I was coming out of the Jewel one night."

"Which Jewel?"

"The one on Chicago and Western. I was comin' out of the Jewel, and—"

"Ain't that an Osco over there?"

"Yeah, maybe. Anyway, I was coming out, and it was Saturday night, and I was carrying my wallet in my hand, and two bags."

"What'd you buy?"

"Some sodas and chips I think. *Any*way, I was comin' out, and I sort of tossed my things and my wallet in the backseat of the car, and then this woman, who was about five feet two inches tall, came over and started asking me what time it was and did I have bus fare she could borrow and stuff like that."

"Was she black?"

"Yeah."

"How big was she?"

"About five-foot-two, smaller than you. Anyway, she walked up closer to me and started acting all sheepish and everything—"

"Sheepish?"

"Yeah, you know, all goofy and embarrassed. Not too sharp. She was acting all sheepish, and I wasn't afraid of her or anything, but then she kept—"

"Was you gonna give her some money for the bus?"

"Yeah, I was gonna give her money for the bus. That's what I was *do*ing, was gettin' some change out of my car, and then she kept getting closer and closer to me, like this."

I got right on top of Tina practically, just for effect.

"So then what!" Tina was dying to know.

"Well, I sort of tried to push her away, and then all of a sudden she wasn't sheepish at all anymore, she was mean, and she said, 'Get yo' fuckin' hands off me!' and then I knew I was in trouble."

"She said that?"

"Yeah, she told me I better get my hands off her. Then she sort of ducked into the backseat and grabbed my wallet, and I was like what the hell, she just took my wallet. And I was trying to *give* her some damn money anyway."

Tina shook her head back and forth as she looked off into that same distance.

"So then what I did was, I backed her up against the car, like this, so she couldn't run off."

I got right up on top of Tina again, like I was in her face, and sort of bumped her a little bit.

"So then what!"

"So then I said to this mugger crack whore freak, I said, 'Give it back!' "

" 'Give it back'?"

"Yeah, I said, 'Give it back!' and then I said, 'Don't take it!' "

" '*Don't take it*'? That's what you said? 'Give it back, don't *take* it'?"

Tina fell into a squat position at the thought, slapping the asphalt parking lot four times with both hands, then standing up and holding her stomach and stomping one foot, she was having such a howling laugh riot. I had to laugh about it, too. It was a pretty darned juvenile response. But it's hard to think of what to say when you're getting mugged, naturally. After it was over, I thought of all kinds of good stuff.

"*Give it back!?*"

"*Don't take it!?*"

Tina kept repeating my brilliant responses, standing upright and catching her breath, then falling down and slapping the asphalt some more.

"Yep, that's what I said. Don't you bet she was scared of me? But I wouldn't get out of the way, 'cause like I said, I wasn't really too afraid of her little short ass. But then she said to me, she said, 'I've got a gun, bitch!'"

Tina stopped laughing.

"A gun? So then what'd you do?"

"What do you think I did? I got out of the way."

"Then what happened? Did she take off runnin'?"

"Yeah, she was bookin' it west up Chicago Avenue."

"Was she really a crackhead?"

"I don't know. Maybe. Or just plain crazy."

"How much money did she get?"

"About eighteen dollars."

"Did you call the cops?"

Finally, when it was getting dark and Tina couldn't think of any more questions, she trotted on home.

When I saw her a week later, she gave me the okay sign, letting me know she wasn't pregnant or diseased. It was later on that night that I saw her rolling around on the side of the court with her chubby, giggly friend. From the talk among the spectators, I gathered that Tina had started the fight, but the other girl ended up on top, and Tina's clothes were starting to come off in the ruckus. Everyone started laughing at her because she was wearing boys' underwear.

The next week, Tina announced she was a lesbian and a poet.

"I'm gay," Tina said, oozing an unstated *whaddya think of that?*

"I think you should be whatever you want to be, Tina."

"Ohhhh, I like that one, she's my type," she said, with lust on her face, looking at a woman walking along the side of the gym. "I like those breasts."

Everyone just kept shooting around.

Tina quit coming to the Y not long after that. Then somebody else quit coming, and another person, until the games started getting unreliable and the Y got to be just like anywhere else. I never saw Tina again.

Looking back on it now, I'm pretty sure I underestimated Tina. Her capacity to lie was one thing, but since the New City Y days, I've learned to be a little less concerned with being taken advantage of, especially by a kid. I don't particularly *enjoy* looking like an ass, and I'll avoid it if I can, but it's not going to kill you. What bugs me now is, I should've taken her to the museum. Probably, we'd have wandered the rooms of the Art Institute, awkward and uninspired in an alien setting, playing roles we weren't accustomed to, relieved as hell when it was over, but that's just probably. I should've taken her, on the outside chance it could've changed everything.

I kept going to the Y on Tuesdays and Thursdays for a while, hoping everyone would come back. One night I was shooting baskets and looking around, and this guy walked over and asked me, "Where'd everybody go?" We shot around, and pretty soon we started playing together.

His name was Randy, and he was a natural coach. He told me once to shoot free throws when I was tired, so I'd be able to make them in the clutch. He was right—the hoop can seem like it's a million miles away when your chest is heaving—but I didn't play in games where free throws were shot.

Randy knew lots of people at the Y, and he started challenging guys to play two-on-two against him and me. We usually won, and he was cocky about it, telling everyone we'd take on any two people in the gym and beat them. Somehow, we just played well together. He stood out by the key while I did most of the running, and that was okay, because I'm a worker bee type of player anyway, and it was a great workout. Nothing is more tiring than two-on-two when you really want to win, because you can never stop moving. I liked playing with Randy, and I found myself starting to look for him when I got to the gym.

Randy wore a wedding ring, and I thought I was just this oddball older white woman he played two-on-two with until one night when something bad happened. We were resting on the sidelines after winning a few games, and he looked at me with this smarmy look on his face and said, "Why don't you wear your hair down for me next time?"

I blew him off with an awkward, entirely unsophisticated snort. I can get like that when I'm surprised and embarrassed. My sheer self-consciousness would be enough to turn King Kong off Fay Wray, but if a guy is looking to involve you in some bullshit, social ineptitude only fans the flames. I stood there stammering around like I was twelve, and then Randy just lost his damn mind and started asking me out more directly, wedding ring and all.

Another asshole. At the time, I was having a rash of them trying to commit adultery with me. I was young enough to attract men, and old enough for them to assume I was experienced and possibly desperate.

I recovered enough to blurt, "Aren't you married?"

He looked at me like that was the most irrelevant thing he'd ever heard. Then he said, "Yeah," like it was a question, shrugging his shoulders.

"How long?" I asked.

"Three months," he told me.

I started asking him a bunch of questions along the lines of "What the hell is wrong with you?" and then I paused, catching my breath and wanting to hear what he had to say for himself. It was stupid of me to let him see I was hoping I'd made some kind of impression on him, because it just gave him another in.

"Would you go out with me if I *weren't* married?" He just had to know, as if he hadn't heard a word I'd said.

I didn't gloss things over for him like some well-mannered Audrey Hepburn type, and I'm afraid he and I quit playing together after that. He apologized every time he saw me, but I didn't believe he was really sorry. He was probably just trying another angle, or maybe he was afraid I was some crazy bitch who might make trouble for him.

A few weeks later I saw his wife, standing on the side of the court, waiting for him to finish up and go home. Or at least she looked like his wife, the way she stood and watched and waited. She was fit and athletic, Lycra- and wedding ring–clad, looking like she had just stepped out of a Spinning class, with her legs all toned and wearing jewelry and makeup, her hair perfectly styled.

I looked down at my pale, skinny legs sticking out from a pair of gray cotton shorts and thought how quickly I would have been discarded by Randy, and how soon he would have tried to turn me into what he already had. *Why don't you wear your hair down for me?*

Pretty soon after all that, I quit going to the Y entirely. The women weren't coming, and I wasn't playing two-on-two anymore, so there was no point. What was I gonna do, take up Pilates?

The bosses at my natural foods job lived in the upstairs of the house where we worked, and they often shuffled down to the offices in their house shoes or involved us in various extracurricular activities beyond dog puke watch. One weekend they were scheduled to move from our walkup to another similar house in the same neighborhood, and we were expected to help, alternately lugging boxes of office supplies and underwear.

On Monday morning Mr. Ponytail made a spontaneous executive decision to paint the new house, and his wife spent much of the day yelling office-related but not pressing questions at him. Cheerfully, he answered back from the top of his ladder, always happiest when she was annoyed.

I decided to go downstairs to the basement for some cases of food I needed to ship, and I happened upon Thonk, the company's resident homeless person, laid out on the floor and snoring between the granola and the fruit leather. The bosses were proud of Thonk. They fed him sports nutrition bars and treated him much like an exotic pet.

When I got back upstairs, Penny the dog had left some recycled Green Strength underneath my chair for me to clean up. Faced with that other-duty-as-described, I went to the bathroom. Ten minutes had passed before I realized I was looking in the mirror, tugging my cheeks and forehead into various contortions and making faces at myself.

I looked out the window at the gray, early March sky. Winter was letting go like an impacted wisdom tooth. My mind drifted to the Wicker Park courts, covered in the sludge that would be there for at least a month.

I needed a vacation. A long one. I started looking for a city to spend some time in, somewhere I'd never been, somewhere sunny where I could find a game. Los Angeles would do. I'd go there.

Visitors' Side

A MIDDLE-AGED, bleached-blond woman stood under a palm tree. She wore gigantic sunglasses and full makeup, and she had on a powder-blue sweat suit, the shiny kind with white stripes up the sides of the legs and arms. A small black dog sat near her, panting. The woman glanced at the ball under my arm and grinned at me as I walked by.

I slowed a little and said hi.

"You play basketball?" she asked.

"Yeah, I do. You play?"

"No," she said, chuckling a little at the thought, "but I think it's cool that you do."

I walked on, cutting through a parking lot where three young guys pushed brooms around, trying to look busy. One of them glanced sleepily over my way, saw me, perked up, ran a few steps in my direction, and stopped.

"Whatcha gonna do with that rock?!"

He grinned and waited to see what I'd say, how cocky I was or wasn't.

"I'm gonna shoot it . . . I think."

"You *think?*" he asked.

"Yeah," I recovered.

"You *think* you're gonna shoot it, huh? Well, I'm gonna come over there and see what kind of game you got. I'm gonna be over there in about five minutes, when I get off work; that's what I think *I'm* gonna do."

"All right then, come on," I said, letting him see me laugh a little as I walked on.

Just past Muscle Beach, there were eight courts, nice ones, regulation size with all the lines painted on and hoops with fiberglass backboards. The courts were surrounded by bleachers, some of them for spectators, and some of them for players waiting to get in a game.

This was it, the shit, complete with a view of the Pacific Ocean. On weekends the play would be so serious I couldn't get in, but the situation that weekday morning was optimal for the approach. People were around, but there was an empty hoop or two. I started shooting, trying to catch a look here and there, being sure to grab any loose ball that came my way and maybe make eye contact with its owner as I passed it back, remembering to try very hard not to miss any shots, in case anyone was watching.

A fortyish-looking guy came over and asked me what was up. We chatted a minute about nothing much, and then he said, "Come on, we'll let you play with us, but don't expect to be treated special now." Of course I didn't.

His name was Sam, and "us" was a bunch of older men, sitting, talking, lacing up their shoes. Sam and I shot around, making it clear we wanted in the half-court game that would inevitably materialize. Others talked and laughed together the way people do when they know each other.

Sam yelled out, "Who's smoking that monkey shit?! Somebody's got some!" Everyone sniffed the marijuana smoke coming from somewhere and laughed.

We shot for teams from the free throw line, and Sam and I ended up on different sides. I was put on a young kid who wasn't very tall or very experienced, and Sam kept telling the kid to mind his basics, complaining when the kid threw a pass away or missed the open man.

Older guys tend to hate it when someone messes up the fundamentals. It's okay if you can't hit the broad side of a barn, but don't just give it away, is how they think, maybe because that's what they have to rely on, not speed or strength anymore, but making damn sure they do the right thing at the right time. The only advantage you can have, when you get old, is mental.

I got by the kid and drove past Sam when he tried to pick me up. When I made the lay-up, Sam looked up to the sky, put his hands on his hips, and yelled, "*Fuck!*" He was mad that the kid had been out of position, and mad at himself for not being able to catch me.

It feels good when you aggravate someone to the point of cursing, but you don't want to make a big deal out of it.

We won the first game and held the court for next. This time I was guarding a guy named Sandy. He had a long, gray beard and long, gray hair, and a black knee brace covered half his leg. I'd seen him earlier, shooting a basket as he whizzed by the hoop on Rollerblades.

Sometimes I feel bad when a game is starting and one of my teammates looks around at the opponents and says to me, the only girl, "You take him." A guy has to know he's getting old when the other team puts the girl on him.

Sandy got set to guard me, sizing me up and nodding a greeting. We lost, and as the game ended, a stinging sensation on the back of my neck reminded me I'd forgotten sunscreen. I sat down on the sidelines, slumped and drained from playing in the sun. Sam walked past me and said, "You tired?" He grinned a little, because I was obviously exhausted, but he waited to hear me say I didn't want to play again before he found someone else for his next game. It was polite of him, and I left, feeling thawed out and relaxed.

I was in my compact, bright red Mazda, stopped at a traffic light on Wilshire, heading west toward the ocean. Past the sea of sedately colored German autos to my right, there was a sudden wealth of grass, an orange basketball flying across a beautiful blue sky. My shoes were in the trunk; I was stopping at Reed Park in Santa Monica.

It was midmorning on a Saturday, and the courts were busy with a bunch of guys trying to get teams together. As I watched from the sidelines, one of the players on the court hollered something, fished around in his pocket, and tossed a coin underhanded to a guy sitting on a crowded bench.

When the guy on the bench caught the coin and sat there, the guy who threw the coin put his hands on his hips and sighed loudly. "Nigger," he said, loud enough for all the spectators to hear him from the court, "put that shit in the meter. You already walked by there twice."

"I'll tell you what I'll do," the other guy said as he stood up and stuck the coin in his pocket. "I'll put that shit in the right pocket meter. Shit."

He waited for everyone to stop laughing before he retrieved the coin from his pocket and bounced it across the court. Meter Guy eyed the quarter, but when he didn't get picked for teams, he headed for the bench and passed the coin by. Then he sat down with the others and lit a cigarette, apparently ready to take his chances with the meter.

As a new game got going, Meter Guy stood up and paced around the bench, holding court until he made everyone laugh and wave their hands and elbow each other.

"You're out of your damn mind and you don't know what you're talking about," he yelled. "Come Saturday night, you'll be wanting someone to pick your ass up!" He was hollering at the guy who threw the coin, who apparently did not own a car, or worry about one.

The topic switched like a crossover dribble, quickly and unpredictably. "Mike Tyson is a nut case!" Meter Guy shouted. "That nigger is mentally all fucked up."

Insanity wasn't, according to Meter Guy, Tyson's only problem.

"And his wife is ugly, too. She look like a pit bull."

Everyone laughed, elbowed.

"You know what, though," Meter Guy continued, looking intently at the man sitting closest to him, who had no choice but to listen, "Tyson's problem is he likes them real bitches that ain't gonna take nothin' from him. He's having his kids with the women he respects, women that remind him of his mama and shit. Shit, they may be mud dogs, but they don't want nothin' from him. Them pretty bitches, they want all the money. Tyson's women, they real."

He turned down his still-audible voice, nodding his head and puffing his cigarette as he looked off into the distance. Clearly, he was thinking about some real deep shit.

Then someone said something about what Tyson must pay in child support, and Meter Guy got excited and started yelling again.

"Shawn Kemp, he had to pay five thousand dollars per month per kid!"

The crowd roared over something someone else said.

"Oh hell yeah!" Meter Guy agreed, sticking with the momentum. "Ain't no way it takes five thousand dollars a month to take care of no kid. As a matter of fact, you really can't spend five Gs a month on a kid. You just can't do it."

His tone of authority was like blowing a whistle, and the group spontaneously divided into arguments about whether or not five Gs could in fact be spent on a kid monthly. On the court, a young guy was trying to fast-break but not getting the pass. He yelled at his teammate, "Come on, baby, please! Shit! Fuck! How long does it take to throw a pass?" He got his pass and made his lay-up.

A big, lumbering white guy, the type who tends to play inside, carry his team on rebounds and defense, and get fouled a lot, was yelling down court, asking someone what the fuck his problem was. His defender said quietly, "Don't take it personal, man."

Faced with advice he should take, Big White Guy became furious.

"Don't take it personal? Don't take it *personal*? You wanna get personal with *me*?" He was just pissed off, feeling like Clint Eastwood and itching to get into it with anyone who'd have some of him. His defender looked away from the emotional mess in front of him and defused the challenge, but on the next play, he guarded the big guy hard, not giving him one inch of a break. You gotta respect that particular kind of manhood.

From the bench, Meter Guy was yelling, "I'm takin' care of the baby, not the baby's mama, know what I'm sayin'?"

He got his uproarious laughing and elbowing. Someone gave him a high-five.

"Fuck that," he concluded.

Somebody's girlfriend sat on the grass, reading a college textbook with a highlighter in her hand. She looked up for a second, shook her head, and went back to reading.

Then someone claimed that Meter Guy had shot four air balls in their last game, and Meter Guy said he'd shot only two. Everyone argued over this matter until Meter Guy yelled out onto the court to get the attention of one of the guys who apparently had some kind of credibility.

"Frederick! How many air balls did I shoot last time?"

Frederick looked up from playing good defense, thought for a second, and said, "Two." Then he went back to playing.

"See there? Shit," Meter Guy gloated.

Shooting two air balls is normally not worthy of bragging rights. Generally speaking, quiet players are better than players who talk a lot.

Meter Guy seemed to notice for the first time that there was an actual game going on. He watched for a minute before yelling, at the last moment before a guy let go of his shot, "You're wide open and you know you're gonna miss!" The ball went up and took a wild bounce off the rim. Meter Guy laughed while the rest of the group shook their heads.

The thing about it was, underneath all the niggers, shits, bitches, and fucks, those guys seemed to have something like a philosophy. To me, Meter Guy, for all his crazy posturing, seemed as real as a Tyson woman. Anyway, I'd sure rather listen to him than some polite conversation where everyone's just trying not to say anything wrong, so they don't say anything really.

I saw Big White Guy another time playing five-on-five with his buddies, all of them white. He was still intense, glowering all over the court as he walked around after plays, but he wasn't out of control this time, and his team was dominating the all-black team they were playing against.

One of the white guys was especially full of himself, yelling and hollering and doing double fist pumps when he did something good. He was feeling it, as they say, playing really well, but the way he was acting, you sort of wanted to see him fall. It's okay to enjoy your moments, but you don't want to take it too far, because after a while, people feel like you're rubbing their faces in it, and besides, it's just unseemly, like you're not that great of a player if you're *too* excited about a good game, or not that smart of a person if you let yourself believe a day's grace is permanent.

Double Pump and Big White were playing on the same team as a balding, vaguely prissy guy in short-short socks who looked more like a rich tennis pro than a playground basketball player. He was good, though, in a competent, by-the-book sort of way. He was in excellent shape, he rarely threw passes away or took bad shots, he worked hard for rebounds, and he tended to neutralize volatile situations because he was one of those people who is honest about making calls. He didn't argue when he was wrong just to get the advantage, and sometimes he'd say, "He's right, it was out on me" or "I got one" when he fouled. I started thinking of him as the Fair Guy.

Meter Guy was back, watching the court and brooding, apparently in the mood that day to let his game do the talking. His buddies sat crammed together on their bench like a bunch of turtles on a log. Five at a time they'd jump off to take on Big White and Double Pump and Fair Guy's team, but no one could beat the white guys.

On one of the losing teams there was a guy with hair braided up in cornrows and beads. The shorts of his matching yellow basketball set grazed his ankles, and he might have been five feet tall with his shoes on. He and Double Pump were into it over alleged roughness, and Double Pump kept saying to the little guy, "It goes both ways, boy." Every time he said it, the little guy answered back so quietly I could hear his hair rattling but not his words. Double Pump kept it up with his "It goes both ways, boy. It goes both ways, *boy.*"

My brother and I used to get in fights like that when we were kids. I'd say, "You're stupid," and he'd say, "I know you are." Then I'd come back with, "You're stupid," and he'd slay me with, "I know you are."

Double Pump and the little guy went on like that until one of the little guy's much bigger teammates went over and said something meant for only Double Pump to hear. Whatever he said, it ended the conversation. Because of the little guy's size, or race, or both, that "boy" stuff wasn't cool.

With every game Double Pump's team won, the bench paid more attention to the play and less attention to that day's bull session, which centered on the question of whether or not J-Lo was probably still creepin' over to Puff Daddy's house. Then Double Pump made this amazing lay-up at full speed, one of those shots where a guy flies past the hoop and throws it in on the way by without even seeming to look and it goes in and it's pretty much a miracle.

Everyone got quiet, gearing up to say the collective *dayyyammmmmm.* But then Double Pump pushed things too far, trotting back inbounds to gloat over his defender just starting to think about getting up off the ground. Double Pump roared like some kind of gorilla, practically beating his chest, humiliating his competitor, and you just had to hate him a little.

Someone from the bench shouted, "Oh fuck you, Scott. I've seen better."

It didn't matter what anyone said, though, because Double Pump kept acting like a Little Leaguer winning the pennant on every shot he made. Unseemly. The other teams started looking for excuses, turning on each other or complaining about phantom fouls, until Fair Guy yelled to the bench guys at large, "It's basketball, it gets a little physical, you ain't made outta glass!"

Fair Guy was a little squirrelly with his bravado, glancing real quick at the bench like he was either frightened he'd pissed them off or hoping he'd amused them.

Someone said to Fair Guy, "Nigger, you been fouling me the whole game." I wondered if Fair Guy would take that word as a compliment, like he was a member of the club, and I was a little relieved for him when he showed he had the good sense not to say it back.

Despite all the heat, everything was okay. Those guys understood themselves well enough to know it gets a little mental, and they really weren't made outta glass, as long as nobody pushed things too far. It's funny how a game can take you to the truth of things sometimes.

I stood in the doorway at Rogers Park in Inglewood, watching the games on a Monday morning. A guy walked up behind me and said what I have to admit I was thinking.

"All these grown men, and no employment."

I turned around.

"Is that the situation?"

"Pretty much," he said. "But hey, they've got good jump shots, and that's all that matters, right?"

I asked him, "You ever see a woman playing here?"

"Every once in a while. They'll let you on if you hustle for the ball." He looked at me for a second before saying, "It's all black, but they'll let you on. You gotta work, though."

The guy hopped into a shiny new SUV and drove away. Inside, the sound of a mean argument over a foul made me think about this court I'd played on once in Chicago, a gym open on Saturday mornings I'd heard about from some guys I played with at Wicker Park. They said some girls showed up there sometimes, and I could play, no problem, so I showed up one Saturday. When I saw all the big, high-flying guys who were there, and no girls, I should've just turned around and left, but I ended up shooting for teams and getting in.

Getting set to play, I tried not to see a guy stripping down to his underwear and changing into his gym shorts on the sidelines. It was unsettling, with all the loud, deep, angry voices echoing off the walls like a foreign language in a place I didn't belong.

I was further brought to my senses during the game, when a player I never saw coming flew from behind and didn't block my shot so much as spike it like a volleyball off my head.

I stood there at Rogers Park remembering that humiliation, and thinking about Lauren, a girl I'd played with in Chicago sometimes. She was good, big and tough, and she didn't seem intimidated by much. One time she was talking about all the different sports she'd played with guys, and she said it was a miracle she'd never had the train run on her.

I guess I looked at her a little funny, like I didn't know what she meant, because she told me: you know, gangbanged.

Damn, I'd never thought about *that.* There was the time I was afraid of that Peter guy in his house, but that was different. We weren't outside on a playground in broad daylight, for God's sake.

It had always seemed that, on the court, most guys thought of me as not particularly fuckable. I've stood by and waited when the game stopped because some girls dressed like girls walked by, making their way around and around the park like floats in a parade, and all the men gaped like they hadn't seen a female in months. With me standing right there.

But Lauren *did* end up getting engaged to a guy who was always taking her to church retreats where she could learn to be dutiful and pray for forgiveness for the times she'd had premarital intercourse before meeting him. So maybe she was sort of crazy and I shouldn't have even listened to her, but that phrase, *running the train,* would just hit me sometimes in situations where rape, like spiking a ball off my head, would be a real effective way to show me I didn't belong.

I'm not out to get into things I can't handle, or ruin a game by turning it into what amounts to four-on-five. It's rude, giving your teammates a disadvantage when they've waited thirty minutes for the court. That day at Rogers Park, with all those men playing a kid's game on a Monday morning, anger and ego were palpable, and I walked on, just like I had good sense.

I was in my car, stopped at a traffic light on Sunset Boulevard, when I saw a mannequin inside the shadowy doorway of a strip club. It was dressed in a bra and panties, posed dramatically with its head down. I was thinking what a good display person that strip club must have to create such a lifelike, stylish effect, when the mannequin suddenly wasn't a mannequin anymore. The woman lifted her head, walked out to the front of the doorway like it was a runway, turned around so you could see her butt in the light, looked sideways for drama, tapped the ash off a cigarette, and strutted back inside the shadows, resuming her pose.

I was trying to get to the Hollywood Y, because someone had told me that sometimes movie stars got a game there. As I edged my car along a few feet at a time, I hoped that stripper didn't have to stand around like that too long, because I myself have had more than one mind-crushing bore of a job, so I could sort of imagine what it must be like to sit there all afternoon thinking, *Fifteen more seconds, and I'll get up and tap out this ash.* It just seems like if you're going to stand around in your underwear all day, it should at least be exciting.

A young kid bouncing a basketball up the sidewalk passed me by. On the other side of the street, a man walked up the strip wearing a long, blond wig, a skintight black miniskirt, and black pumps. All his makeup made him look old and not less unfeminine, and it made me a little sad, thinking about him leaving (in my mind it was reluctantly) wherever he lived for the bright light outside. Then the traffic light turned green, and I stopped and started my car along past him.

There were two separate gyms at the Y. On one side there was a bunch of movie-star-looking-men-in-the-prime-of-their-life playing five-on-five, shirts against skins. There was a chalkboard where you signed up for next, and a few dozen men hanging around on the sidelines. Forget it.

In the other gym some little kids were playing a three-on-three game. They looked like they were about seven or so. One side was wearing Junior Laker jerseys, and the other side was in street clothes.

The best player was a Hispanic boy on the street clothes side who could shoot a lay-up and actually dribble. The ball tended to find its way to him, and all the other kids on both teams seemed to think the idea was to run to wherever the ball was and try to get it, whether they were on offense or defense. It looked like they were playing five-on-one, and the Hispanic boy was winning.

There were parents sitting on two benches, but no one looked like they belonged with the Hispanic boy. Nobody cheered especially hard when he scored.

The one girl who was playing seemed more interested in taking her hair in and out of a scrunchie than playing basketball. She wore blue jeans and a white T-shirt with a pink, glittery butterfly on the front, and when she got the ball, she'd run for about five steps before she began to dribble. The refs, who were doubling as coaches, didn't make many traveling calls.

The girl kept looking over at her dad all through the game, and he'd tell her things to do. He was serious about it, like it was really important for her to do well. Every time the girl got ready to shoot, she picked up the ball, ran around for a few seconds as she looked up, brought the ball back to her ear, smiled, then heaved the ball in the air. Her shots made it about halfway up to the hoop.

The Junior Lakers had a short, stocky boy with a seventies-style mushroom haircut and a constant grin on his face. When he found himself with the ball, he widened his eyes really big, like he had no idea what he might do next but he couldn't wait to see what it was.

The kid's obvious dad had a long, gray ponytail, and like the son, he appeared perpetually on the verge of laughing. He kept looking at the other parents, the way you do when something funny happens in a movie and you want to see if the person sitting next to you thinks it's funny, too. But the other parents didn't seem to notice him, riveted as they were to the sight of their own kids

competing. I liked that smiley dad. At least he wasn't trying to re-
live some disappointing aspect of his youth or Tiger Woods his kid.

Another Junior Laker had dark, allergic-looking circles under
his eyes, and he kept glancing around at all the other kids, like a
chorus-line dancer who hasn't memorized a routine. The look on
his face said the best he hoped for was to get through the game
without drawing too much attention to himself. His tall, skinny
dad paced the sidelines bouncing a basketball with a grim look on
his face. He wore a rattling watch chain that clanked every time he
moved, and it was impossible not to notice him, with his rattling
and his bouncing. Every once in a while, he would take a loud and
clanky mock jump shot. Then he'd stand flat-footed and practice
his form, shooting the ball into the air and bending his wrist with
good follow-through the way coaches always have you do. You
could tell by the way he handled the ball he'd played a little.

During a timeout, the rattling dad took his kid aside and gave
him pointers as the rest of the kids surrounded their coach. When
the dad finished up his lecture, he threw the ball really high into
the air, almost to the ceiling. It was a little sad to see the kid throw
his hands up over his head and duck, in his fancy Junior Lakers jer-
sey, as the ball came back down.

There was nothing for me at the Y, so I decided to take one of
those tours of the stars' homes, just for the heck of it. As I walked
up Hollywood Boulevard and turned the corner onto Vine, it was
like there'd been a set change; suddenly, I could've been at any
American theme park.

People were overweight again, wearing their khaki shorts and
running shoes and sunburns. The same "three T-shirts for ten dollars" deal was being offered all up and down Hollywood, and many
of the shops sold commemorative plaques for various movie stars
or miniature Oscar trophies that said "World's Best Dad." One
store sold refrigerator magnets and nothing else.

I walked over to the van, and as my fellow tourists and I settled
in for the ride, two women and a man from Ohio laughed and told
everyone how they'd just called one of the women's husbands and

told him they'd seen Jennifer Lopez in Frederick's of Hollywood, which they hadn't. The wife, who looked to be about a size 18, carried a tiny pink Frederick's bag. She said she was starting to feel a little bad for her husband, because he'd gotten so excited about Jennifer Lopez and had kept asking questions about what she looked like. "He likes her," she said with a shrug.

I guess that's love, indulging someone's juvenile preoccupations, instead of despising him a little, and squeezing into whatever was in that little shopping bag.

Our tour guide, Jim, swung into the driver's seat. He shouted "Welcome to Hollyweird!" and we took off.

"This is the house of Brad Pitt!" Jim screamed over the air conditioner of our van. "That is the Brad Pitt house, right there, the one by itself on the cliff! Then Brad Pitt he had the lady stalker in the house, so he took her to the court and he forgive her. Now he live in Beverly Hills, where they have the securities and the service secrets."

Jim told us he was a Greek from France who had moved to Hollywood fifteen years ago to become a movie star. He had the looks for it: not strictly gorgeous, but with the requisite straight teeth and thick hair.

We worked our way back up Sunset for a while after viewing the house of Brad Pitt. "Lots of crazy ladies here, the prostitutions!" Jim hollered as we drove up the famous street. "There you see some crazy ladies in the night," he said, pointing out two very tall and wildly dressed people, possibly women, sauntering down the sidewalk. He showed them to us as if they belonged to the city, like they were statues or public buildings.

"You know the actor Hugh Grant?" Jim screamed so we could all hear. "Here is where he was caught with a prostitutions. Right at this corners! And he has a beautiful girlfriend. He say he want to be with a black crazy night lady. I do not understand." Jim laughed like someone who exists in a mad, mad world.

As the van groaned up into the Hollywood Hills, Jim showed us the house of Steven Spielberg, which was visible from a mile away.

"He owns the whole hill to himself. He doesn't want the neighbors! Ha ha!"

Our attention was directed toward the garage of Shaquille O'Neal, where he housed his fifty cars. *Fifty* cars. I mean, really, couldn't someone *cure* something with all that money, or put some poor kids through college or something? Maybe Shaquille O'Neal should just make enough money to afford, say, six cars. That should be enough for anyone.

My mind wandered to thoughts of a couple I'd seen with their kid at the park a few days earlier. I was dribbling a ball around, which is a good way to see people when they don't know it. The couple walked, holding hands, their child bounding around them, to a grassy area, where they tossed a soccer ball on the ground. As they started kicking the ball, they laughed, involved, moving, not watching or worried about being watched. They seemed to be onto something. Most people I see can't be that happy and relaxed, even for a few minutes, with the people they live with.

Nobody cares whether or not a family kicks a ball in a park, just like nobody cares if I play basketball. We're not paying money, or watching commercials. It's pure.

So I don't totally trust professional sports. And anyway, watching basketball on television just makes me antsy, makes me want to play. And I hate to high-five; I really hate to high-five over something happening on television with people I don't even know.

Then again, maybe I'm just a stubborn jackass. It's hard to say.

Jim led us back to Sunset. He showed us the Laugh Factories, where the biggest and funniest comedians in the country played, like the Bob Sagets. Then we passed the Hustler, where you could find to buy some spices to put in your relations, and the bathroom where George Michael the crazy man from England got caught naked.

"Here is the place where Eddie Murphy the black comedian was caught with a male prostitute!" Jim screamed delightedly. "He say he was just giving him a ride, but they don't believe him and they take him to jail! Eddie Murphy, Beverly Hills Cop!"

"It's easy money in the movies!" Jim hollered at us. "Not like me, driving a van every day to pay the thousand-dollar rent. Ha ha!

"Here is the house of Ella Fitzgerald, the black jazz singer from New York, she battle the prejudice," Jim yelled at us. "And there is Walt Disney, a shy guy from Missouri who became a millionaire through a cartoon character, the Mickey Mouse! His neighbor is Rod Stewart, the singer from England I am sexy!"

When the tour was over, I got out of the van and walked back down Hollywood, nearly tripping over three giggly guys taking each other's pictures by Sylvester Stallone's star. I was thinking again about that happy family kicking the ball, and the miserable kid in the gym with his clanking dad. As usual, I was busy living in my head with the people I wish I could be more like and the ones I worry about, which was just one of fifty good or not-so-good reasons I wasn't walking around with a Frederick's bag or calling someone back home to play a joke on him or say I love you. That, and I don't high-five when the situation calls for it.

A Weeble-shaped Hispanic guy with a mullet haircut was getting ready to toss the jump ball for a junior high girls' game when I stuck my head in the door to see what was going on at Hollywood's Poinsettia Recreation Center. I watched the guy say something that made the girls giggle before I headed back outside, where there was a full court and two smaller half-courts, and a handball area nearby.

On one of the half-courts, two women were putting a group of girls through some drills. The girls ran laps around the court for a while, and then they performed pivots, over and over. I watched them and their coaches, who ran and pivoted, too. They looked a little like synchronized swimmers, with their arms going up and down and their legs swinging around all together.

Over on the full court, the game looked serious. There was a crowd watching, talking and laughing and touching hands and saying hey.

There were a couple of teenage girls hanging out on the sidelines, wearing serious basketball clothes, knee-length shorts and sleeveless jerseys in no-nonsense colors, with their hair up in this or that funky way. I was hoping to see them get in, but they didn't. They only jumped in to shoot a few while the game was on the other end. Sometimes one of the guys standing nearby would chase the girls around or put some spontaneous defense on them. The girls laughed and showed off with some flirty moves. Then they'd get out of the way as the game came back down.

A game on one of the half-courts looked potentially ragtag, so I walked over to watch. One team had a guy who was so much taller and bigger than everyone else that all anyone had to do was lob the ball somewhere in his direction and the other team was left jumping at him like gnats. Pickup ball is often pretty lax about the three seconds in the lane rule, but the big man ignored it entirely, so he shot as many times as he needed to get two points. He didn't even need to jump.

Two guys walked up and called next. I told them I wanted in, too, and they said okay. We chatted a minute, and I found out they were UCLA students. One guy was German. His name was Heinz, he said, just like the ketchup.

We watched Big Man's team annihilate their opponents, and then we picked up a guy off the losing team to play four-on-four. Our new player was a tall black kid, as skinny and cool as the Pink Panther, and just as silent. He gave a quick nod when Heinz asked him if he'd play, and then he jumped up to the rim and hung on, swinging there while the rest of us organized ourselves.

Pink Panther took Big Man, who outweighed him by at least one hundred pounds. We didn't have a chance.

Big Man took a lot of notice of my being on the court. As we played, he'd say stuff to his teammates that was really meant for my benefit, stuff like "Don't let her fool you, stay on her!" Then he'd yell "Double!" every time I put the ball down, even though I wasn't traveling, and if I took a shot, he'd say "No shot" just before I let go of the ball. He was trying to get into my head.

Once I made the mistake of dribbling too quickly after a rebound, moving away from the hoop with my back turned, and Big Man thundered out from the post, double-teamed me along with my defender, and stole the ball. It was the first time I'd seen the guy hurry.

Big Man and Pink Panther looked like a straight line bumping into a circle, and pretty soon Pink just gave up trying to defend Big and began to focus entirely on his offensive strategy, which was to shoot every time he touched the ball. Even with his sorry 10 percent field goal percentage, he scored most of our points. Heinz and his friend and I worked our butts off and managed to score a few times, but it was inevitable that we lost, six to eleven.

Afterwards, Heinz invited me to stay around and shoot with them, but I was ready to go. I guess I looked a little defeated, because after Heinz said good game to me, he added, "Hey, six to eleven, at least we didn't get doubled." He was a nice guy, that Heinz just like the ketchup.

I ducked my head back inside the gym as I was leaving. The girls who had been doing the jump when I got there were between games, and I watched a coach-dad give one of the teams some quick tips on defense.

"I don't want to see nobody guarding nobody else outside this line," he said, slow and loud, running the toe of his shoe along the three-point line. "And I don't want to see no three people guarding one player with the ball either."

His post player turned a spontaneous cartwheel.

In the small lobby area just off the court, there was a humble-looking bulletin board with the heading "Girls' Sports Rock!" Pictures of everyone from Billie Jean King to Anna Kournikova were pinned to the board, getting across the message that it's okay to be a dyke, but you can still enjoy sports even if you're not one. There was an article about Chamique Holdsclaw's bad childhood, about how her parents fought and drank and raised hell, and how she'd go play basketball to get out of the house. "All the boys would groan when she followed them out onto the blacktop," the article said.

Then I walked on. In the middle of an open grassy area, I saw one of those teenage girls with the fancy basketball clothes. She and a boy were off by themselves, sitting together real close in the grass, and her demurely bowed head smoothly contradicted all the different ways adults try to convince girls that sports rock.

It's an uncommon female who's willing to fly alone above the junk, keep her head up, and let the boys groan, if that's what they need to do. It's not hard to see why. In some ways, it's easier just to shut up and paint your toenails.

There was a game going on at Roxbury Park in Beverly Hills, and I have to say, things didn't look too serious. The most noticeable player was a mentally handicapped guy running up and down the court and never touching the ball unless it landed in his hands by accident. He wore a yellow Lakers baseball cap facing frontward, which marked anyone as not serious in my book. You don't play with your hat on right if you plan to shoot. You can't see the hoop.

The teams were loosely divided between black and white guys. The black team had two players almost as rotund as Big Man at Poinsettia, but these two biggie-sized dudes were shut down, because the game was full-court and they stayed so winded they could hardly keep going.

The black guys looked like they were in their midtwenties. Two of their friends were sitting on a bench on the sidelines, goofing off and watching the action. One of them had a towel draped over his head, like he'd been benched in the pros.

The white guys were mostly teenagers. I kept noticing one of the white players in particular, a short, skinny, blond kid wearing an oh-so-urban knit cap that fit close to his head. As soon as I saw him, I thought, *Well, would you look at this little 90210 punk?* Like I knew anything about it.

A white guy walked up and asked who had next. When I said I did, he scowled. He shot around for a minute on one of the empty hoops, and then he went over and started slanging it up with the two black guys on the bench. When they laughed a little at something he said, he seemed to puff up a little.

I watched the game for a while until the score was tied at game point and one of the Biggies got an open shot under the hoop, which he somehow managed to miss. Then he got the rebound and missed again. I don't know how he did it. There was no one even guarding him.

The two bench guys laughed at the first miss, and when Biggie missed the second time, they started hollering and shoving each other. Then, when Biggie #2 got the rebound and he missed, too, the guys nearly fell off their bench, they were laughing so hard.

The teenagers finally lucked into a rebound, and the Biggies lumbered after the fast break, walking. They glanced over at the bench, and when they saw their friends laughing at them, the Biggies smiled and shook their heads and waved them off. I admired their sense of humor. It's not easy to laugh at yourself when you're fat, exhausted, and getting beat.

Then the white team managed to miss the open lay-up on their end, and it was like watching a bunch of really dumb people try to end a game of Trivial Pursuit. The rebound went to the Lakers cap guy. Of *course* it went to the Lakers cap guy, who stood flat-footed, looking down, shocked to find himself with possession of the ball. He was wide open from the corner of the free throw line, and he threw the ball up with an underhanded granny shot. As the ball sailed toward the basket, one of the guys on the black team — the only one who still cared about winning — shouted, "God*dam*mit!" like he knew the game was over.

And it would've made perfect sense to lose the game like that, the way things were going, but the shot didn't go in.

The black team got the rebound. The Biggies, who had only made it to half-court by this time, turned around, looked at their own hoop, and began moving back the other direction like two forlorn barges.

Another dude wandered up and started talking to the bench guys about what had happened with this girl he'd just been trying to get with. He was giving an elaborate and detailed play-by-play, standing directly in front of the bench so he was impossible to ignore, with his cornrows and Hawaiian print shirt and wild gestures. The two guys had to look around him to see the game, which was only just now absurd enough to be interesting. Finally, one of the bench guys asked the new guy, "Well, how'd you end the conversation then?"

Sensing he was losing his audience, the new guy looked over at me and met my eye. I was just sitting on a bench with a ball in my hand.

"Hey, Sheryl Swoopes," he said, "All right." He flashed me a big mack daddy smile and seemed to freeze, like he was posing for me to take his picture.

"I bet you kick all their asses."

I laughed and told him it was doubtful.

The game *still* hadn't ended. "Man, one of y'all get in here," Biggie #2 was begging the guys on the bench.

Had he been a horse, someone would have shot him, but the bench guys were merciless. They waved him off and said, "Nawww, man, I ain't playin'."

After another play, Biggie #1 said just forget it. He walked off the court, and Biggie #2 followed. The white teens shouted, "No way! Come on, dude, finish it up!" But it didn't matter. The Biggies were going home.

I walked onto the court and shot around, along with the guys who wanted to play another game. Some others approached, and it looked like things were going to get more serious. The guy wearing the Lakers cap was gone, the Biggies were long gone, even the bench guys had left, and new teams were starting to form.

I was using a women's ball that none of the guys really wanted to shoot with. They seemed not to want to be associated with the smaller ball, like it was a tampon or something. So I just kept shooting and shooting.

To be frank, I wasn't in the best mood ever. I kept seeing the scowl of that slangy guy so anxious to be in the cool club that he treated *me* like a tampon, and I started thinking *fuck it* with every shot. Or maybe it was *fuck you* that I was thinking, but in any event, I was making everything.

There were fifteen people out there, so some of us weren't going to get in. Someone asked the punk dude with the skullcap if I was their fifth. He glanced over at me and said, "Yeah, she's with us."

I was impressed, because I'd watched him play earlier, watched him work hard, hollering at the Biggies to stay in and finish their preposterous game. He liked to win, and he could have easily said no, I wasn't on their team. He could've gotten the best guy available instead of me. But he knew that would have been dissing me, because I'd been there the longest and I had next, even though I wasn't asserting it very well. So he didn't do it. I admire players like that, guys with character who take what the game gives them and make the best of it. It's pretty Zen, when you think about it, acceptance and not trying to control outcomes and all. It seemed like everything that kid was made of was right there, in four barely considered words. *Yeah, she's with us.* Had I just passed him on the street, all I would've known was 90210 punk, a stupid prejudice based on a meaningless cap.

I love this game.

Walking past the tennis courts at Venice Beach, I saw a girl in a bikini playing doubles with three guys. My speculations regarding how much money someone would have to pay me to play tennis in public in a bikini were less compelling after a woman Rollerbladed past me in a thong.

I made it to the courts, and before I could get my ball out and walk over to a hoop, a guy who was shooting around said, "Hey, sexy lady in gray, you wanna play? Come on."

He was black, with a shaved head. I made the usual quick judgment and decided he was probably harmless with his ridiculous "sexy," but, fearing the specter of enthusiastic hand checking, I didn't want to play one-on-one. So I laughed a little and said, "Well, I'd like to shoot around, if you want to." He said okay.

He said they called him Plato, and before ten minutes had passed I'd learned a good deal about his past, which included five kids by three different women and a variety of complicated custody arrangements. Plato was convinced that a person needed freedom. It just got old, he said, two people waking up together every day, looking at the same face all the time, fighting about money and ruining everything.

A man walked by and hollered, "Best thing that ever happened, Plato, gettin' married!" The guy kept going, never slowing down, and Plato gave him a quick thumbs-up without a hitch in his talking and shooting. A few minutes later, the guy walked by again. "Best thing that ever happened!" he shouted, still smiling, heading off to the other court.

Plato was telling me about the birth of one of his children when another guy walked up and started shooting around with us. I said to the new guy, by way of including him, "We're talking about having kids. You have any experience with that?"

His name was Clem, and he had a sister and some nieces and nephews, so he knew a thing or two about a thing or two. He and Plato promptly fell into an opinionated debate on epidurals.

Clem said he was thirty-seven, an actor and screenwriter working as a nighttime security guard. Plato never said what he did. Since it was the middle of a weekday and he was playing basketball in cloth high-top Chuck Taylors, shirtless and showing off an outstanding chest and flat stomach that almost no office-job-having man could maintain, I guessed he must have had lots of time and not much money, so I didn't ask him about work.

When Clem and Plato started up about the roots of basketball, I felt like they were putting on a show for my benefit as a guest on their court. Plato told the story I'd always heard about Naismith and the unruly YMCA kids in Connecticut. Clem said no, that's what everybody thought, but it wasn't true, and they argued about that for a while. But no topic other than sex could last very long with Plato around. He started in about some past exploits with one of his old girls or something he was going to do with his new girl.

Looking embarrassed and like he wanted to change the subject, Clem mentioned he'd just seen the actor who played the Pretender on television. He said he'd seen a lot of famous people at Venice and had actually played with Woody Harrelson when he was there doing research for *White Men Can't Jump*. According to Clem, Harrelson was a hack player, but the movies could make anybody look like they had skills.

I wondered aloud about all the people who made it and didn't make it in LA, how one person had her face on the side of a bus, and another ended up in a strip club doorway. Plato's theory was that the difference was made by what actresses were willing to do to get parts. Then he stared off into space for a minute, like he'd forgotten Clem and I were there.

"Psssht," Clem snorted, before Plato could say something cruder. "The entertainment industry isn't the only one where people sleep their way to the top. And anyway, they don't want you to be *too* perfect-looking. It's really about personality, charisma."

Clem said "the entertainment industry" a lot. He was in the business.

"Yeah, look at Sandra Bullock," I commented, expertly.

"Exactly," said Clem, taking a shot. He said "exactly" a lot, too.

"And she's got that nose," he added, scrunching his face like he smelled something bad.

Plato rejoined us from his casting couch reverie. "Who? Sandra Bullock? Oh, she's cute. What they want is someone who's pretty without any makeup, people who are just natural," he said, cutting a quick glance at my obviously unenhanced breasts.

"They want somebody real and wholesome, like Melissa here. Yeah."

Plato grinned, studying my face as if he was appreciating it because of what he'd said, or maybe just to see if I was convinced. But I was thinking about a guy from Chicago who used to say I was a "wholesome little Arkansas girl," just like Plato did. As if we didn't have sluts in Arkansas.

Then they started arguing about what made Robin Williams a genius. Clem said he worked at it all the time, and Plato said it was just a gift, talent.

I thought it was probably a combination of both, and that's what made it so rare, but I didn't say so. They seemed to be enjoying their argument.

A twentyish-looking Latino guy walked up and hovered a little, just like Clem had done. Plato saw him, grinned, and said, "You got the shoes, but you left your ball at home?" The guy was wearing a sparkling new pair of the latest Kobe Bryants. He started shooting around with us, hitting everything.

Clem and Plato and I kept talking, but Kobe Shoes wasn't there to contemplate the nature of comic genius; he was ready to play. He gathered up a couple more guys, and we shot for three-on-three teams. Plato and Kobe Shoes were on a team, Clem and I were on a team, and each team had two big white guys wearing T-shirts with their fraternity letters on the front.

Since Plato was such a hard-body, I was surprised to hear him grunt like an old man getting out of a chair with every long pass or rebound. He was older than he looked. I was guarding Kobe Shoes. He wasn't that tall, but he didn't need to be, because he could shoot from the outside, and he was super-quick. If I guarded him too close, he'd go around me, and if I backed off him at all, he'd nail a jumper.

About all I could do was box out and try to keep him from getting rebounds, which I did, but the other two matchups were even, and the game was largely decided by the difference between Kobe and me. My team lost.

Before a new game started, everyone stood around in a circle checking out each other's footwear. A guy came over from another hoop, more interested in finding a conversation than a game. He looked at Plato's cloth high-tops.

The new guy said, "Man, I don't know how you play in those things."

But then he said the best shoes he ever had were an ancient pair of leather Converse All-Stars. He talked about those old shoes like a first car or a girl he shouldn't have broken up with.

Everyone had a lot of questions about the Kobe Bryants. Kobe Shoes mentioned he worked at Champs and got a discount. He said "prototypes" a lot. I suspected he was good at his job, good at everything.

After another person walked up, looked at Plato's shoes, and said man I don't know how you play in those things, Plato treated us to a demonstration, performing a quick shuffle but not turning his ankles too much, keeping his feet straight out. And, he said, he wore three pairs of socks for ankle support.

Finally, two teams organized themselves for a new game. I said I'd play if they needed someone, but otherwise, I was out. I wasn't too anxious to guard Kobe Shoes again, to tell you the truth. I didn't really mind being outmatched a little, but Kobe Shoes was just too good. If I was on him, my team was pretty much guaranteed to lose.

"Come on," Kobe Shoes said. "Play, it'll challenge you."

Here's the thing. Insecure guys like Mr. Tampon at Roxbury worry about playing with a girl, like it makes them look something less than studly. But if a guy is confident in his game and in himself, he's more likely to welcome a girl, or an old man, or a serious young kid. That's how Kobe Shoes was. He loved the game, and what he saw in other players was more than their shoes or their skills.

They had enough to make their teams, and I was glad to sit down for a while and watch. A new guy wearing huge mirror sunglasses quickly sank four shots from past the three-point line. On the fourth bomb, Plato stopped everything, leaned over, put his hand on his knee, and said, "What the . . . ?!"

Of course there wasn't an answer. The guy was just on, and he laughed it off in good form.

Clem the actor had taken on his lane-dominating persona. "Don't you come in here no more!" he'd yell at someone on the other team, indicating by his outspread arms that the lane was all his. Then he'd laugh at his own absurdity.

A few plays later, Clem hurt his arm and shouted a prissy "Dammit!" He got out and came over to sit by me. After a minute or two, here came Plato to sit down, too.

They started talking about their child-rearing theories. Childless Clem said he would kick them in the ass when they messed up, and prolific Plato said no, you can't hit them.

"When I was a kid and got in trouble, I had to go outside and cut my own switch, and I'd always try to get a medium one," Plato said. "You didn't want to get one too big, but you sure didn't want to get one too small and have them go back out and pick one for you, huh-uh, no way."

Since I practically knew Plato's entire life story by now, I was aware that his parents were from Arkansas and Oklahoma. I think maybe that switch-cutting routine is a southern thing, because it's a story I've heard a lot of my relatives tell. Every time I've ever heard it, the person focuses on the dread he felt when he had to go cut the switch, and what strategy he used to pick it. I never heard anyone tell about the actual beating.

Plato paused for a minute, thinking, before he said, "You know what? That's some real fucked-up slavery shit right there." He said it like it was the first time the idea might have occurred to him.

Clem said oh hell, he used to get beat with extension cords, like it was nothing.

"I've got this brother," Clem said, "and he's always talking about 'Remember when Dad did this' and 'Remember when this happened' and constantly bitchin' and moanin' about our childhood. I say, 'I don't even remember that stuff, and if you're letting your childhood wear you down, then you're more fucked-up than you think.'"

"No, man, it's like baking a cake," Plato said. "You've got to know what all the ingredients are before you can make a good cake. Your brother's just trying to understand his childhood, that's all."

Plato was getting calmer, while Clem was getting more and more agitated. Even though the two men were about the same age, Plato seemed eons older.

Clem said no, fuck that, the goddamned cake was already fucking baked, and the ingredients didn't matter, goddammit. They kept arguing, sounding more and more like they were talking about actual cake, until they suddenly stopped, looking confused.

I was with Plato, really, but I didn't say so.

"Well, you got to get over that hitting thing, anyway, before you have kids," Plato said to Clem, smiling at him in a way that closed the topic and could only be called kind.

The short wall we were sitting on backed up to a grassy hill, and Plato leaned back on one elbow and gazed off toward the tennis courts. His new girl's birthday was coming up, and he was gonna get her some cake, yeah, mmm-hmmmm, yes he was, cake.

He mumbled something about some plan involving candles. Clem and I tried not to hear.

I hung out a little longer, watching the new game and listening to Clem and Plato throw in their two cents' worth about walks or fouls.

Three young and pretty Asian girls walked by in a slow, look-at-us kind of way. One of them wore flip-flops, scuffling them so that, in case you hadn't looked yet, you'd be sure to hear them coming.

I expected Plato to make one of his risqué comments, but instead he snapped out of his sexy trance and said, "Girl . . . pick up your feet."

Men in their late thirties might be my favorite. They've still got it goin' on, but they've quit thinking with their penis at least to the extent that they are capable every once in a while of avoiding women whom they know will be purely irritating. The combination is attractive, a foot in both worlds, a kind of peak.

When I said I had to go, Plato rose and grabbed the back of my hand to give it a kiss, all gallant. I looked past him and gushed ridiculously to amuse Clem, but only a little; I didn't want to hurt Plato's feelings. The smile Clem gave me was neither prissy nor tough, just real, a glimpse at what was behind all the roles he played.

That kind of glimpse never lasts long. By the time I'd gathered up my things, Clem and Plato were debating the difference between an ape and a monkey. As I walked off Plato gave me an offhanded wave, never looking, never missing a beat.

With pickup ball, it's always about the game, but sometimes it's also about fleeting intimacies the game makes possible.

If Venice Beach nights were for the old guys, afternoons were for the studs. As the early risers finished their play and their talk and began to leave, the testosterone rose with the temperature.

I was sitting in the bleachers one early afternoon, munching a burrito and watching the transition. The concrete courts and the ocean spanning out from them were beginning to sparkle in the sun, and I was pleasantly tired after playing with the oldsters all morning.

A hip-looking guy in dreadlocks yelled at a guy on the other team.

"You sorry-ass bitch!"

The crowd around me giggled, bored and a little lazy in their flip-flops and hungry for action. A small boy with Down syndrome and his grandmother climbed up the other end of the bleachers. The boy, in cornrows and a shiny miniature basketball uniform, stayed in front of the grandmother, using his hands on the bleachers to make sure he didn't fall down. He kept looking behind him and cowering a little, like he was afraid he wasn't moving quickly enough for the grandmother, who never released him from her calm, threatening gaze. After they sat down, the little boy looked relaxed.

"You sorry bitch!" Dreadlocks yelled again. "Take the ball, with your bitch ass!" He slung the ball at the other team.

Clem was back, playing on Dreadlocks' team. He was a young oldster or an old youngster. He could mix.

Clem had good fundamentals, starting the offense every time from the low post with a hop to the other side of the lane and a screen. Again, I noticed a vague effeminacy about him. His screen hops were on the sassy side, and when he shot a jumper, he stuck his butt out real far and had extra good follow-through, leaving his bent wrist up in the air and bouncing on his toes.

Almost every time Clem missed a shot, he'd stop the game with a call, leaving everyone on the other team looking at each other and complaining, "What was that about?" Calling fouls just to get the ball back is about the lowliest thing you can do in pickup basketball. It's not like refs are there to keep things fair.

Clem kept making the calls until the other team was yelling at him, and then he started yelling back. "Blah, blah, blah, give us the *god*damned ball!"

Then the crowd would laugh.

Once, when Clem had brought the game to a stop yet again, the point guard from his own team looked at his defender and said quietly, "I don't know, man. He's a pussy."

"Toot it! Toot it!" the little Down syndrome boy yelled, anxious for them to stop standing around.

Dreadlocks got so mad at the sorry-ass bitch that he forgot who was on his team, and he threw the ball to a guy standing on the sidelines. The guy had his fishing gear strapped to his back, a long pole bobbing over his head, and he caught the ball with one hand.

"Dude! I'm not playing!"

"Shut up!" Dreadlocks countered, and then, after thinking a second, "Eat your hotdog!"

The guy wasn't eating a hotdog. He threw back a solid pass and said, "I've got your hotdog, slim."

The crowd thought that was funny, too.

A young, curvy Latina walked by, wearing ultralow-waisted jeans and a short T-shirt that showed her flat belly. Her pants were so long and flared that you couldn't see her feet, making her look like some kind of urban mermaid spray-painted on a wall. Her boyfriend walked ahead carrying a surfboard, and he couldn't see her when she grinned at a good-looking guy on the court who was slobbering over her. It was one of those thunderstruck moments, and everyone could see what was going on. Except the boyfriend, who just kept walking and carrying his surfboard.

They walked on down the beach, and it took the good-looking slobbering player a few minutes to shake it off and remember where the hell he was.

Earlier, I'd asked one of the old morning dudes why they argued so much in LA. He told me the younger guys got into it when women were watching. In the hot sun with their shirts off, the players seemed like posturing lions, desperate to stand out.

Clem was yelling at the court at large, ever ready to philosophize. "You know what your problem is? All that testosterone gets going and fucks you all up in the head!" He squinted his eyes tight and flashed his teeth as he said it, using all the fingers of one hand to tap his own skull, like the whole thing was impossibly frustrating.

I hated to admit it, because I liked Clem, but he really was playing like a pussy.

The little boy stuck his arms up in the air and called out to the guys on the court, "My turn, pease! My turn!" but the players weren't aware of his existence. The grandmother ate her nachos and stared ahead, looking vacant.

The fisherman dialed his cell phone and left somebody a message that he was at Venice Beach, home of the freaks. Then he hung up and resumed standing there like some grinning statue.

Many of the tourists in the bleachers were smiling, too, but the little boy and his grandmother and the small group of black people they sat with watched the game as if it were a rerun of a television show they didn't particularly like, but there was nothing better on.

A ghostly white player wore pants and long sleeves and had his shaved head covered with a bandanna. Amid all the dark skin, the colorless guy looked like an alien protecting himself from uninhabitable conditions. Once, when he and Dreadlocks collided and fell, the crowd drew a collective breath, like they thought someone was hurt and they were afraid, or maybe hoped, there was going to be a real fight now. But Dreadlocks extended a hand to help the pale guy up and said, "You okay?" quietly, passing his brown hand over the guy's smooth bandanna like he was stroking a baby's head.

Men are strange that way. One minute they handle each other like they're pulling legs off bugs, the next minute they're tender as nurses. I guess there's a hell of a lot that goes into it, how their relationship to each other seems beyond their control as they respond to the call to compete, like the lions.

After the game, Clem and Dreadlocks sat together in the bleachers, and I saw that human smile of Clem's again, now that he wasn't acting out some drama. On the court, an old Frederick Douglass–looking dude was trying to get in the next game, and all the players were ignoring him like he was a little kid under their feet. FD was wandering around the court, asking people who had next or did they need somebody, and the guys would mumble, "I don't know, man," and turn their back to him. But the old dude stuck it out, and by the time another game got started, he was in.

The kid who was put on him looked awkward with the association, and a couple of hipsters sitting behind me in the bleachers amused themselves by making fun of how short the old dude's shorts were. What was strange was, the shorts were fine, really, I mean, they weren't Magic-Johnson-in-1976- or Bill-Clinton-jogging-short-short. They were too insubstantial to be stylish, but exactly what you'd expect from an older dude. I guess the peanut gallery needed something to chew on.

The poor old coot didn't play very well, even for an old guy. He looked dazed, a few seconds behind everyone else. He wasn't at all like Sandy from the morning, gliding up to the court on his Rollerblades, saying little, and playing like a sage, everyone asking him how he was doing and saying thanks to him when they left. Instead, FD was in over his head. His team lost the game and the court without much question about it, and I felt sorry for him, after all that work to get in.

A deformed pigeon pecked around for food in front of the bleachers. Where one of its feet should've been, there was a round, marble-sized mass, and instead of strutting like a proper city chicken, this one wobbled like a broken rocking chair. Or he simply stood, by himself, looking up at us in the bleachers, red, crazy eyes demanding something.

I felt a sudden urge not to be sitting in the middle of a crowd by myself, but the bombardment wasn't over yet. On the way out, I passed a group of middle-aged, retarded men arriving at the beach. They were so perfectly silent I could hear their shuffling feet as they moved by, holding hands like little kids on a field trip. They were being good boys, smelling vaguely of Lysol and staring up at the sky as if they'd forgotten it was there, and my crazy head couldn't help wondering how they were treated back at the institution, whether or not somebody was nice to them.

Pease, said the child who scrambled up bleachers like a nervous crab. Please, I said, slinging the word like a half-court buzzer shot at anything that might be called God. Please help the old, the hobbled, and the innocent, forever begging the strong for crumbs of gentleness.

On good days, you approach a court, and even if you don't know anyone, it seems like everyone has been waiting for you to arrive. Players are well meaning and intense and amusing, and you go home feeling like the world is a pretty good place.

It was often that kind of day at Westwood Park. There were teenagers, college guys, some families on the half-court side, even a girl or two sometimes.

I was there shooting around, waiting for a game. A very pregnant woman and her toddler walked past me, and I heard her ask the child, "You wanna go play *bas*ketball?" They went over toward a hoop, and the little kid started throwing a small ball up into the air. The mother clapped her hands, paying attention to the child and nothing else in the whole world.

A guy in red shorts shooting at the hoop near the toddler kept catching my eye and smiling. Another guy came over to my hoop, and we shot around. His name was JJ, and he was in for the day from Pasadena. I mentioned to him I'd just bought a new ball, because I'd lost my old one. I said the ball had been on sale for fifteen dollars, and I was glad to get the deal, because all the other balls were twice as much. He laughed a little and said well, he would've gotten that one, too.

Westwood was a neighborhood full of Mercedes- and BMW-driving UCLA students. I didn't realize that my talking about saving fifteen dollars was a little different before JJ's slightly amused and gentle reaction.

The game on the other court ended, some of the guys were leaving, and the remaining players looked around for replacements. JJ and Smiley Red Shorts guy and I looked over, showing our interest, and the guys on the court included the three of us in the head count, no big deal. In the world of pickup ball, this was an advanced civilization.

JJ said his knee was hurt, so he didn't play. The rest of us started a game of full-court four-on-four.

Most of the players were students, and they worked hard without taking themselves too seriously. The best player toyed with whoever was guarding him, challenging but not humiliating. When he faked you, he smiled a little at the subtleties of your response, and when he got you off-balance, he might or might not take it to the hoop. He tried to teach you something, not saying much except little things like "Whatcha gonna do?" and "I thought so" and "Uh-huhhh."

He'd found a way to keep things interesting for himself while at the same time letting you have your game, but he turned it on a few times, too, to show everyone he could.

A tall blond guy and I went for a loose ball, both of us getting our hands on it. As we tugged for possession, he shouted, "I love you!" and we laughed. Finally the ball got away from us, and we gave each other an absurd and dramatic fast hug. Throughout the rest of the game, his eyes danced when he looked at me, seeming to revel in my oddball freedoms.

I was guarding Red Shorts guy. Something about his initial smiliness had made me think of him as a little soft, a little underconfident and too anxious to please. When he turned down an open shot, I knew I was right about him. After a few hesitations like that, I backed way off him, physically daring him to shoot, but still, every time he was open, he'd study the hoop, then pass. So I said what you say when your guy won't shoot.

"You better take that."

There are certain times when you don't shoot even though you're open, like when you're not in your range, or you can't get your balance in time, or no one on your team is under the hoop to get your rebound if you miss. There are exceptions, like when you just have a feeling it's going to go in. Then you take the shot, even if it seems wrong-headed. If you miss, you feel like an ass, unless you're a ball hog and don't care about anything except shooting every chance you get.

When your man backs way off you, it's a disrespect move, like you're not worth guarding, and your man actually wants you to shoot, since you'll probably miss. When a defender lets you have the open shot, you better take it, just to get some respect.

I could tell by the look on Red Shorts' face that he wasn't feeling it, he almost never felt it, and I was making him feel some pressure by calling attention to him. Pretty soon, my teammates would start noticing what I was doing. Then they'd jump in, too, saying things like "He ain't gonna take that" or "No shot" when he got the ball. Red Shorts needed to shoot and say, "You don't wanna let me have that," just before he let it go. That's what he needed to do, no matter how he felt.

When Red Shorts finally took his shot and missed, I felt a little powerful, and a little guilty. I mean, he was so friendly and everything.

Our best player was a short Asian guy with muscular calves who could take it through the lane even though he was smaller than most of the other guys. He was strong and quick, he could jump, and he got lots of steals for us, but his contributions were offset by a ball hog on our team. Like all ball hogs, for this one, defense was no more than the boring end of the court, and rebounding was for suckers.

Being the smallest person out there, I had little chance for the offensive rebound, so as soon as Ball Hog shot, I got back on defense and tried to cause the other team to miss their shot on the break. If they'd miss just one, my teammates would have time to get down the court, but on the first few breaks, my team didn't even try to get down, leaving me to guard two or three people by myself, jumping and sweating and jerking like those old Western movies where someone shoots a gun at your feet and says dance.

My inner guy wanted to say, "Shit, y'all! If I'd known you were just gonna let 'em *have* it, I'da stayed back, too! Why don't you leave me back here running my ass off by myself next time? Shit!" But I knew I didn't have to say anything, because guys feel sheepish about letting a girl work hard while they loaf. Pretty soon, they started getting back on defense, especially the Asian guy.

We had most of the same people for three games, with a few substitutions here and there. JJ from Pasadena couldn't resist getting in when someone had to leave. He was on my team.

JJ was an excellent player, and he didn't like to lose. You could tell by a slight grimace on his face and a give in his step he was pushing his hurt knee too hard, and he complained under his breath, about his knee and about Ball Hog's shots. Once, when Ball Hog threw up something crazy, JJ looked over at me and said, "I wouldn't be takin' that." I shrugged in agreement.

A loudmouth white kid was on the other team. He had a military haircut, small, squinty eyes, and freckles, and he was guarding our ball hog, a short, stocky black guy. Pale and dark, tall and short, thin and fat, young and old—the only thing these two had in common were a couple of extra-large mouths.

Ball Hog kept telling the Kid he looked like a vegetarian. "You'd better go eat something, that's what you better do. Go have a carrot," he'd say.

Being called a vegetarian is not the most debilitating insult I've ever heard on a basketball court. And the worst part was, the Kid wasn't even abnormally skinny, just your garden-variety basketball lanky. Ball Hog was breaking one of the unstated rules of talking trash: if you're going to dis someone for what he looks like or what he's wearing instead of his playing, you better be right on target with it. If you're going to take the focus off the game, you better be saying what everyone's already thinking, that's how right you better be. Otherwise, you just look cheap.

The Kid made some stellar passes, and Ball Hog said, "We know you can pass, but can you shoot?" Only someone demented by ballhoggedness would say such a thing. Ball Hog's rap was just off, along with his game.

After a few more trips up and down the court, it was obvious that Ball Hog was way out past the buoys. The Kid was pretty good, a foot taller, younger, and in better shape, with fresh legs to boot. Ball Hog began to talk less, and the Kid began to talk more.

JJ filled the silences that inevitably followed Ball Hog's failures and the Kid's tirades with, "Come on, guys, let's D up and win this." Our team was losing because of Ball Hog, but we followed JJ's example of solidarity.

The more deflated Ball Hog got, the more aggressive and full of himself the Kid became. Once, after they ran the ball down and scored on us yet again, the Kid yelled, "What are you doing down at the other end waiting on a pass for? Why aren't you down here with your team playing defense? You know, *de*-fense?"

Ball Hog had in fact been loafing on our end and waiting on a down-court pass, as usual, but the ball had gone out of bounds, making it obvious that everyone else on our team was already back on defense. He walked toward us, keeping a steady gaze on the Kid, who had gotten into a hard-core defensive position, his knees bent, his arms and hands looking like they were ready to make a steal, rocking on his feet a little.

"*De*-fense! You know, *de*-fense?!"

The Kid was gleeful, trying to turn us against Ball Hog by saying we were working harder than he was, which we were. But we stayed quiet as Ball Hog took his punishment and the Kid worked himself into a frenzy.

"What are you doing down there? Waiting on the Kentucky Fried Chicken truck to come around? Why don't you just let your team run while you sit on your butt and eat yourself a big, juicy piece of—"

And that was it. Ball Hog had had enough, and in a flash he was in the Kid's face. Actually, Ball Hog's face was in the Kid's neck, but that didn't matter, because it was on, now. "Look," Ball Hog said, sounding lethally in control in the wake of the Kid's shrieking, "you don't know me."

It was code for "Don't get too familiar, white boy." Ball Hog had chosen to interpret the chicken comment as a race thing, but as for myself, I wasn't so sure. I mean, Ball Hog had been saying all the skinny vegetarian stuff, so maybe the Kid just thought he'd talk about meat and make fun of Ball Hog for being on the chubby side. Ball Hog himself might not have believed the comment was racist. He could have just been using it as an excuse to get the attention off his playing and scare the Kid into shutting up. Or maybe the Kid really was bringing race into it. I don't pretend to have the answer.

The thing is, on the court, you *do* know people, because you've all played the same game. Even if you've never seen someone before, usually you know his type after a few trips up and down, or even before the game starts. JJ and the teacher dude were like fathers, the kind too few people have, the wise and cautious kind. Ball Hog was an always-drunk uncle everyone puts up with.

The Kid looked down into Ball Hog's face, not saying a word, his tiny eyes nothing more than slits. He was scared, and he wasn't sayin' shit. Then he started stammerin' around, mumbling something about "What? I don't know what you mean. What are you talking about?"

JJ said, "Come on, guys, let's get it, let's win this."

The rest of the game was played quietly, and we lost, and I walked away thinking about how, as wrong as Ball Hog was about some things, JJ had stuck with him. JJ wouldn't leave Ball Hog out there hanging by himself, even though he didn't like the way he played, even though you might say Ball Hog deserved abandonment. That's because we were on the same team, and to me, that felt like family, no matter where I was.

Home Court

I WAS REVIEWING a contract with the ponytail boss. He'd just finished telling me how he was a better harmonica player than Junior Wells when I felt an explosive, snorting laugh welling up in my chest. I excused myself and went to the bathroom.

After a minute or two, the sound of a fist banging on the bathroom door was inevitably followed by the lady boss's shrill voice.

"Melissa! You have a phone call! Are you going to be a while, or are you just taking a pee?"

"Just a minute, please, can you take a message?" is what I hollered back through the door, leaving my coworkers, who were all within earshot, to draw their conclusions about what was taking me so long.

It was a day much like any other.

I kept working and haunting my favorite courts, and then it was winter, and I found myself standing on an El stop platform waiting for the Blue Line. The temperature was a balmy zero degrees Fahrenheit, but the negative-seventeen wind chill factor made it a little brisk outside. We'd awakened to what would be the first onslaught of the largest snowstorm that year. The trains were running late, and as I waited and waited and more and more people crowded the platform, I began to suspect the trains weren't running at all.

We hung on, second by second, desperate as landed fishes. Those of us with any remaining fortitude ran back and forth from the platform to the ticket booth, demanding the CTA worker call and find out where the goddamned Blue Line was.

FROSTBITE.
FROSTBITE.
FROSTBITE.

The word flashed on and off in my head like an electronic scoreboard ad, and I noticed that I was crying as I hid my face in the faux fur collar of my warmest coat.

Just have to dress for it, my ass.

It was around then that a friend introduced me to a friend of a friend, a guy who lived in Arkansas, and we began a frenzied exchange of e-mails. When I asked him if he played basketball, he said sure, he would run the hoops. What we had in common was nearly nothing, but a generous reality dose had lowered the Sterno on the buffet of urbanely sophisticated Chicago men. After four years away, Arkansas was shrouded in the warm, friendly glow of fantasy.

All I really knew about the friend of a friend was that he had a good voice on the telephone and a good vocabulary in his daily e-mails, and he came recommended, but I enthusiastically included him in the glow.

I visited a time or two. We said all the stuff you say about love and building a future. In the early springtime, I decided I would move back home, because the winters were getting to me. That's what I told myself and everyone else, and it was the truth, but not really the whole truth. It's easy to find a reason for something you want to do anyway.

Our "relationship" survived the harsh light of physical proximity for one and one-half weeks, until he said he loved me but he wasn't "in love" with me, and what he really wanted to be, he guessed, was a satyr.

A satyr. That's what he said.

When a guy starts to talk that double talk, you have to lose him, sure as if he tries to throw you out a window. You just can't put yourself through it unless you want to be stuck singing "I Will Survive" and trying to mean it.

We were in Satyr's apartment, and just before the love but not in love he was *carrying* me, and you know I hate that, but I let him do it, because I didn't want to give him a complex. But God, it's awkward when men think they're supposed to haul you around all over the place, and you have to watch out and make sure they don't crack your head on any door facings and ruin their big cinematic moment.

By the time Satyr finally got me in the bedroom and gave me a tepid heave-ho onto the bed, he was huffing and puffing like a freight train, which would have still been okay if we could've laughed or something. But we didn't.

Then he started kissing me all passionately, then telling how he loved but wasn't in love, and then kissing me some more and making his face look all sensuous, but by then I didn't believe his words or his face or his carrying or anything. I didn't even believe myself when I said whatever it was that I said to him.

The whole episode was pretty jolting, after one and a half weeks, as you might assume.

In the middle of all the chaos, Satyr looked at my arms. I was wearing a sleeveless shirt.

"You have nice arms," he said. "They're like the opposite of the night sky."

What he was referring to was that I have freckles. It was a freckle rap.

"What?" I responded, blinking a little like a sleepy frog caught in the beam of a gigger's flashlight.

He pointed to one particular freckle and said, "I want to go there."

Then it was back to the love but not in love.

He had a stifled grin on his face, like he was nervous but still enjoying himself. Then he'd get very somber and dramatic and stare off into space and be very reflective and concerned, like I was somebody's leg that had to come off, what a shame.

It was some bullshit, and I had to leave, right then. But I can tell you I was getting pretty tired of having to beat it out of some man's apartment and drive home all shaky.

Back home, with my living room full of moving boxes and the need to go out there and live the good life staring me down, I got a little depressed over the whole satyr fiasco. No surprise there, but then I just kept on being kind of depressed, too depressed to go out and find a new good job, look up a friend, or even play basketball.

I was pretty sure I was clinical and needed help getting back to my usual state of low-grade pissed-off, which, if highly imperfect, was a lot more interesting than my new hobby of lying prone on the floor and staring at the ceiling. Thinking back on all my romantic exploits, I wasn't too high on myself. After a while, it just occurs to you, *Maybe it's me*. It was most disturbing to think I was actively involved in finding the confluence of inanities that seemed to stalk me.

Wanda Mason, LSW, was listed in the yellow pages, and from my first appointment with her, I had her pegged as seriously Christian, because, being in Arkansas, there was a real good chance of it. Also, she had the Serenity Prayer and a number of other religious sentiments cross-stitched and framed in her office.

Wanda asked me some questions and had me do some personality tests, and at the end of our first hour, she suggested I spend the next week reading *Women Who Love Too Much*, which she loaned to me.

The book's pink cover pictured a very reflective-looking woman and her big, feathered hair. A single long-stemmed rose was designed into the words of the title, seventies-style. The photography was soft-focus, and everything was pastel, in the manner of feminine deodorant spray packaging.

The pages were yellowed and coming loose at the spine. A collection of different handwritings filled the margins. Clearly Wanda had loaned this thing out a time or two.

I spent the next day reading dozens of case studies of women who loved too much.

> Tammy was a well-dressed and attractive forty-year-old college professor with expressive hazel eyes and a Ph.D. in anthropology. She had been dating her boyfriend, an unemployed screenwriter with a drinking problem, for two years, during which time he'd had affairs with three different women, including her sister.

The margins had men's names handwritten and underlined four times with an angry face, or "that's me" written small, with a sad face. I got depressed all over again with that book and its crazy writings. It was like looking up from reading a newspaper to discover you've been riding the emotional little bus for a very long time.

"In session," Wanda's favorite move was the surprise question. When she was ready to make me have a breakthrough, she would suddenly blurt, "Are you ready to be different? Are you sincerely ready to change?" I knew she was trying to get my buy-in or commitment or something, and that was probably part of therapy, but when she asked me, I would just nod a little. I couldn't bring myself to say, "Yes! I'm ready!" like I knew she wanted me to. It was the same feeling I got from the socially expected high-five. I mean, I can high-five when I feel like it, but I can't do it just because I'm supposed to. I guess I'm not that enthusiastic sometimes. But I didn't blame her for trying. You have to fake it, a little bit, just to get started.

So, instead of acting like everything was going to be okay, which Wanda had made as easy as saying yes, I started rambling on about Satyr, my favorite topic of discussion. In the middle of one of my many statements beginning with "I just don't understand why he—" Wanda interrupted with another question.

"Do you feel like your biological clock is ticking?"

I think she was a little bored.

I wasn't worried about any clocks. Instead, Wanda's question made me think about this little boy, Xavier, who I saw one time in the *Chicago Sun-Times.* The paper advertised a baby for adoption on Wednesdays in a little space called "A Family for Me." On Tuesdays and Fridays it was pets from the animal shelter, on Mondays it was chess moves, and on Thursday it was needlepoint techniques.

I cut out Xavier's ad and kept it for a while. I can still remember it. "Meet Xavier," it said. "It looks like this sweetie pie has discovered his toes, and he is waiting for you to discover all of him! Xavier, three, loves for you to talk to him. Others say, Xavier is becoming a regular little socialite who enjoys playing with others in their playpen. What you can do: You can spend lots of time with him!"

Xavier just looked mostly confused to me, at least in that one picture of him I had. One day I threw the ad away, but then I just kept remembering his face, and I got the ad back out of the trash. I wasn't going to save Xavier, but somehow it seemed better if I didn't forget him either.

This was around the same time that women using fertility treatments to put things in God's hands were having six or seven kids at once and getting their pictures plastered all over the covers of magazines. Entire towns were dropping everything to change all those corporate-sponsored diapers, while Xavier sat by himself confused and lonely and got his picture taken to run in the newspaper with the stray dogs and cats.

Those litter families would be on the cover of *Good Housekeeping* again on the kids' birthday. You could always tell who the littlest one had been when they were born, because he would be wearing thick glasses or a hearing aid or have cerebral palsy or something, and the article would say what a great job he did using his walker to keep up with his brothers and sisters. Usually, they put a big present or some other prop in front of him, or had him being pulled in a wagon.

I just thought someone should be thinking about Xavier instead of a biological clock, that's all.

And then I kept thinking about David and his mom, the ones back in Wicker Park. I could never forget that one small moment when David's mom picked up her dribble and looked at him, and he smiled and looked back. You could see his eyes widen and his body rise up a little bit, like he knew something good was about to happen. He actually seemed to grow a little taller when his mom looked at him.

I wasn't sure I could be that way, that I could be a part of creating a life so good like that. So having a baby was the last thing on my mind, with little kids like Xavier sitting there already born and everything, and considering that my romantic relationships were characterized by embarrassment and brevity. But something told me Wanda wouldn't interpret my reflections on Xavier or David as a sign of robust mental health, so I didn't get into all that.

I just said no, I wasn't sure I wanted to have children.

Wanda scanned her shelves, looking at me with a sidelong glance that said, *I'm not sure they wrote a book for this one.*

She changed the subject.

"What makes you happy?" she was dying to know, and I thought about playing basketball until it gets dark. Back home in the driveway, we'd rig up a big lightbulb on the side of the house, hanging it by a nail and using an extension cord to plug it in, so we could keep playing. Or that time in Chicago, when they called me Little Larry Bird, and I was still hitting when it got too dark to see the ball coming anymore. Or nights at Venice Beach, the sun disappearing into the ocean, people leaving for the day with their surfboards and fishing poles, stopping for a moment longer to watch people playing for a moment longer.

Maybe happiness is having something you don't want to leave when you have to. I went home, pulled out a moving box, and started looking for my ball.

TO STRENGTHEN FAMILY, FOSTER COMMUNITY, AND GLO-RIFY GOD. It's painted twice—once in English and once in Spanish—on the glass doors going into the Jones Center in Springdale, a town where newspaper classified sections are loaded with eviscerator, catcher, and de-beaker career opportunities. The more closely a chicken factory job resembles a medieval torture process, the better it pays, so people hustle to get on at the plants. Someone told me once that the factories don't let anyone work too long in the killing rooms, because they're afraid it will warp somebody's brains after a while, maybe make him go off the deep end and do something to cause the chicken company to get sued. I don't know for sure that's true; it's just what somebody said. But it wouldn't surprise me a bit.

The Center was a gift to the community from Harvey and Bernice Jones, an ancient, childless couple who made their millions in trucking, not chickens. It has a pool, basketball courts, an indoor track, a weight room, and an ice skating rink. There's a chapel that doubles as a movie theater, and about a million paintings of Harvey and Bernice hanging around. There's also a life-size bronze statue of the two of them set up all by itself with a velvet rope around it. He's wearing overalls and an engineer's cap, and she's in a dowdy dress and sensible shoes, just like regular folks.

Lots of Hispanic people work at the chicken jobs. Some Springdale natives like to make little comments about how many Mexicans ride in a car or live in a house, you know, coming-out-the-windows-type stuff. The way they say it makes it sound like God's country is teeming with immigrants, nothing to worry about as individuals, but all together a swarm taking over things, one chicken-plucking job at a time.

It makes me so sad to think about the people in those plants all day, trying to keep everything new and hopeful while they're swimming in gore and wearing hair nets, doing jobs nobody wants to do and being resented for it. So I like Harvey and Bernice, even with their "glorify God and look at my statue" gig, which would normally give me a big pain. I like them because they had some Spanish painted on the front door of that place, and that's important in a town like Springdale.

I still wasn't strictly ecstatic on life. There was some junk in my trunk, as they say, but it helped to be playing, to walk up and assert myself, to move and forget things.

I was at Jones one day, playing with a bunch of white dudes. We'd been there for a while, and even though we were still divided into teams, we were really just messing around, most of us tired and getting ready to think about leaving. I was probably the most tired of all, having just come back from my hiatus and everything.

When a group of Hispanic guys walked up, called next, and asked what the score of our game was—all entirely proper protocol—one of the guys in our group perked up and started grinning and cocking his head to the side like a confused dog. He looked around at those of us on the court and started asking what the score was 'cause he didn't know what the score was, did anybody know what the score was.

Now, when a group calls next, they've got next, and that's all there is to it, unless it's just ridiculous, like a bunch of second-graders trying to play against teenagers or something. But these were just regular guys, and there was nothing ridiculous about it. They had next.

People often act sheepish or confused right before they do something mean. It's a common tactic I've noticed. But this ringleader dude, he was acting a little *too* sheepish, like he wanted the Hispanic guys to know he was screwing with them, just to see what they thought they could do about it. He was inviting his fellow whites to laugh, too, with all that winkety wink wink.

Nobody really joined in with him, but nobody was calling bullshit either, so I said, "It's eight to ten. Y'all're up."

That's what I said, but I didn't know what the score was or what we were playing to.

"And we're playing to fifteen."

I knew better than to look at Ringleader. I knew he'd be a little pissed at me for answering the Hispanic dude's question like that, and I hadn't been away from a certain kind of southern boy for so long that I didn't know exactly how he'd be looking at me, still grinning, but with something new and mean and vivid dancing in his eyes. I was afraid I'd lose my nerve if I looked over at him and he looked back at me. I was afraid I'd add something meek and disastrous to what I'd said, something like "I think."

I tried not to look at anyone at all, but for just a second I locked eyes with the guy who'd called next. His barely perceptible nod felt like an acknowledgment, but who knows; maybe I was just another Caucasian looking for a thank-you. What I do know is, the guy who'd called next stood on the sidelines keeping score, loudly, as we finished playing our bogus game. He held his ground, watching, making sure his team got its turn, and I was proud of him, or as proud as anyone can be of a complete stranger.

After being ready to quit, everyone on the court was hustling again, trying to get rebounds, swearing at missed shots. I played hard, too, my legs burning with fatigue, and I steered clear of Ringleader, imagining how wild his elbows might get. The good ol' boy glee bouncing in his eyes felt a little slippery, like it could easily morph into something else, and I didn't need any "oh gosh did I get you in the nose I hope it's not broken" crap.

Playing with Ringleader wasn't what I'd call high-quality basketball. You have to wonder if some people ever have anything really good, even for a day, even for a minute.

Something happened one time years ago when I was playing Pictionary with a group of people, all of us white. The game was close, and nearly over, and a guy was drawing something that could've been interpreted as a big head of hair.

The rules are, you have to guess what the picture is before time runs out, and the person drawing can't say anything.

"Afro!" somebody yelled.

The guy drawing shook his head no and kept trying. The sand was running through the miniature hourglass, and everyone was hollering out answers, laughing and hectic. A group of people playing a board game on a weekend night: nothing but pure wholesome entertainment, right?

The guy who guessed Afro must have thought he was hot on the trail of the right answer, because he kept shouting out guesses, and we all laughed louder with every shout.

"Black!"

"African American!"

"Bill Cosby!"

Then he did it.

"Nigger!"

I was pretty sure the guy didn't think that would be a legitimate answer on a board game. He just said it to see if everybody would keep laughing when they heard it.

Some people are always fishing to find out where you stand on important issues of the day, see whether or not you're like they are. They think about stuff like that *all the time,* even when it has nothing to do with the situation, but since they can't very well introduce themselves by saying, "I hate niggers, don't you?" they just throw out some bait and see who bites.

None of the Pictionary players did, and the host didn't hesitate before saying, "We don't use that word in our house." The room got quiet, the sand finished running to the bottom of the miniature hourglass, and nobody guessed the right answer, which was porcupine.

The guy scrambled to recover before managing to assume a studied air, like he was thinking of something real deep and was gonna try and explain it so as we'd all understand.

"When I say *nigger,* I don't mean *black.* I know white people who are niggers, too."

It wasn't the first time I'd heard this bit of redneck intellectualism. It's a basic part of the toolbox for someone who wants to keep saying *nigger* all the time but still thinks of himself as a nice person.

I grew up around that kind of thing, in a town where there were no immigrants and the only black people who ever came to our house were some guys who worked for my dad at the furniture-making factory in the next town. Dad was a line manager there, with blacks working under him on the line and whites working above him.

The line guys came over to play basketball in our driveway sometimes, and it tended to raise eyebrows. The neighbors didn't say anything—it wasn't like the Klan lived next door—but you could see their cars slowing down a little as they drove by the unusual sight.

My dad liked to see the cars slowing down. It made him proud, like he was taking a stand against all the rednecks in the world, including certain of the white bosses, aka the "big shots," wearing their short-sleeved shirts and ties, talking about *paperwork* in a way that made the word sound as complicated and mysterious as quantum physics, shaking hands with each other in church, and telling what they considered to be hilarious stories about the last animal they shot, how some raccoon's body acted without a head.

My dad had a job with paperwork, but he didn't go to church and he didn't hunt. Most of the time, he was just solitary.

The line guys drove the ten miles out to our house together, and my brother and I went out on the driveway to shoot around with them as they and Dad figured out teams. If they needed one, they picked up Andy, and as they took the ball out for the first play, I went to the edge of the garage, put the tailgate down on the El Camino, and sat down to watch. It was assumed that I didn't get in when the line guys were there.

The line guys were good players, and so was my dad. He was around thirty-five at the time, and he was barely five-foot-nine, but he was fast and creative and bold enough to drive the lane and get his share of inside shots.

He still had some of the old high school point guard in him, apparently impervious to the three packs of Salem Menthols he smoked every day. He was a passer, ready to hit you upside the head if you weren't looking, and he played hard defense.

My dad didn't smile very often. He didn't like for anyone to see his teeth, because he had an overbite. I had the same teeth, and I remember one time before I got braces, I was laughing and some older kid stuck his top teeth out to show me how I looked like a dorky beaver type of person. That certainly caused an abrupt end to my good time, and I could see how my dad wanted to avoid it, but out there with the line guys he seemed to forget about his teeth and the rednecks and the big shots and his factory job and his loneliness and whatever all else he thought about. Out there on the driveway, he was laughing and hollering like players do, because the game was always good when the line guys came around.

Sometimes my dad would tell Andy and me about the time he set his high school record for scoring, about how, when he was playing, no matter how loud the gym got, he couldn't hear the crowd. It was still one of the highlights of his life, one of the places where he found peace, I think.

He was happy to play with the line guys, who had grown up playing, happy with the way they told funny stories instead of corny jokes, the way they didn't spit tobacco or make you nervous talking about did you know where you were going to spend eternity.

The line guys were some of the few people who made my dad

forget to hold his face in check, and I wish I could say I grew up in a house where nobody ever said *nigger*. Life is hardly ever simple, is it?

My brother Andy and I still play together sometimes. He knows his way around a pickup game, and it's nice, showing up at a court with him. We usually get on the same side, but sometimes if there are a lot of players and everyone shoots for teams, we end up on opposite sides. We never want to guard each other, though. It's awkward, trying to keep him from scoring, and neither of us seems to try very hard when we're matched up.

Andy, his friend Brett, and I had been shooting at Jones for a while when I ducked my head around the vinyl curtain separating the two courts and saw these three young guys. They looked a little alike, all rawboned, with angular, fatless bodies, pimply faces, and greasy, peeled-looking hair. They were just standing there, so I asked them if they wanted to play.

One of the guys said, "You sure?" all cocky like.

"Yeah, I'm sure," I said.

"Are you *really* sure?" he asked me, grinning, like he thought it was pretty funny, me taking them on.

I said, "Yeah, come on," giving him less of a smile than he gave me.

We started playing, and the guys were good: experienced and fast and strong. There's no way the game should've been close, but somehow it was, and we ended up winning. The rawboned guys didn't like it, getting beat by thirty-year-olds, one of them a woman.

"It's that crappy ball," the cocky one said. "We don't wanna play with no fake NBA crap. Where's that other ball at?"

The other ball was actually the bad one, an old leather junker that never should've been taken outside, but it was Andy's ball they were calling crappy. It was a disrespect move. And a lame excuse.

Andy laughed casually and said, "Yeah, well, let's switch 'em out." Then he and I walked over to the water fountain, cool as salad. But once we were out of earshot, I looked around to make sure those guys weren't coming and admitted to Andy that I thought we were pretty lucky to win that one game.

Andy's face was red, and his shirt was soaked with sweat. He's pretty fit, but the bottom of his T-shirt hung away from his shorts a little, giving away the distinctive over-thirty proportion you see on the court. He rose up from the water fountain and said, "Gotta go!" like he was going to head for the exit and leave me there.

Our asses got good and kicked in the second game. It was a regular testosterone fest, although Andy and Brett's version was a little tamer than the rawbones'. I wanted to win, too, trying to be intense in my own way, with everyone around me dripping machismo. I kept my game face on, knowing Andy and Brett would expect me to. I didn't smile too much or put my hands on my knees to rest between plays or anything.

After they beat us, the young guys looked relaxed and relieved, like their world made sense again.

"Yeah, well, wait till they're thirty," Andy said, laughing, as we packed up to go.

After that game, most every time I went around Jones, I'd see some of those guys who beat us. One of them worked at the desk, and when I'd get a ball, he'd yell out to another worker, "Don't give her no ball, she ain't got no game!" just like that, the same exact way, every time. I'd always laugh for him, or sometimes I'd mumble something about him putting his money where his mouth was. It seemed like the right thing to do.

But I didn't say much, because I really don't talk trash very well, like I said. Some people find it easier to live in the moment, enter the milieu of social discourse without even thinking about it. They wouldn't call it "enter the milieu of social discourse" either; they'd just say what they were thinking and then probably forget about it ten minutes later. Me, I remember what I didn't say for years.

Andy always knows some guys playing somewhere. I think it's because men invite each other to golf or play basketball or be on a softball team. I get invited by women to Pampered Chef parties, which are probably fun and everything, but when you go you're expected to buy something, and I never seem to have an extra twenty-five dollars in my budget for a new baking stone. I already have enough baking stones at my current inventory of zero.

For a while, Andy and I played together at a middle school with a group he knew. One day I got there early, and I'd barely pulled my sweats off when two nine-ish looking girls came running up to me, asking if they could shoot my ball. I said sure and tossed it over to them.

It was clear from the get-go that most of the talking would be done by the pretty one, an exquisite-looking creature with a long, straight, blond ponytail you knew guaranteed her a life of friends and envy. Her sweatshirt was a perfectly faded navy blue, and it hung to just the right length, and it wasn't too baggy or too tight. A personal stylist could have lived in her bedroom, working full-time to make her look accidentally perfect every day.

The two girls were about the same size, skinny and bristling with imminent transformation like tadpoles sprouting legs, but their physical similarities ended there. The friend had dark, coarse, unruly hair. Three inches of wrist stuck out awkwardly from the sleeves of her garish pink sweatshirt with a cracking, silk-screened rainbow covering its front. And her face was disfigured, especially around her nose and eyes, where her skin looked like it was stretched too tight. I imagined her born that way, with some "condition" or "syndrome." In my family, old ladies would have said she was a mongoloid the poor little thing, and the nice kids would have said don't look at her, she's retarded, our word for all conditions, even those, like hers, that appeared to be physical only.

The disfigured friend suggested a game of horse while the pretty one bounced around looking like a Basketball Barbie Junior. I said a game of horse sounded fine, and the friend shot the first basket and made it. I shot, and I made it. Then the pretty one hurriedly shot and missed.

"What does that make me?" the pretty one asked, her eyes darting toward the door.

"H," the friend and I said.

The friend shot again. She made it.

I shot and missed.

"H," the friend and I said again.

We told the pretty one that now she picked her own shot, and the friend passed her the ball. She caught it and shot an airball from where she was standing.

"H-O," she said.

The friend and I tried to explain to the pretty one why she didn't get a letter, but she wasn't listening. Instead, she was trying to convince her friend to go outside and talk to a boy for her, to find out if he liked her. The friend refused on the grounds that she was afraid the boy would beat her up. Actually, she seemed interested in our game of horse. She really looked at the hoop when she shot; she concentrated on making it. The pretty one asked me if I would go outside with her, and I said oh no, huh-uh, I didn't mess around with any mean boys.

Of course, I've messed around with plenty of mean boys, but I was trying to make them think they didn't have to.

"Just make me H-O," the pretty one said, tossing the ball absently in my direction.

As we played horse, I gathered that the pretty one felt like the boy outside had led her on, saying he liked her until she started liking him back. She kept squealing, "I'm so mad!" Then she'd make an exquisite little stomp with her foot, and squeal again.

"Boys don't like me," the friend said with a shrug.

I said something about them being nice girls (I almost said pretty and I should've said smart) and not to worry about anything. They sort of listened, but I could tell by the way they looked at me that it was clear to them I wouldn't know anything about it.

Other girls their age were coming around, looking excited to be in the pretty one's crowd. They were jittery and quick-moving, following instructions.

Andy and some other guys wandered in, and the group of girls disappeared outside. Maybe they were pursuing the boy, with their newfound safety in numbers, but whatever it was they were doing, they looked like they'd accomplished it when they came back. The pretty one marched her group over to the bleacher where Andy and I were sitting, waiting on the next game. She asked Andy if we were going to have the court for a long time, and he politely told her yes, we were.

She squealed and stomped before turning back to the charges standing all giggly and shy behind her. She indicated to her entourage that they were to form a circle, and they began their own game just off court, where everyone else in the gym, all teenage boys, grown men, and me, couldn't help seeing them.

The game had simple rules. The pretty one threw a basketball straight up in the air, as high as she could. The girls clapped once, and the pretty one caught the ball. She threw it up in the air again. They clapped twice. She caught it. They did it again, clapping three times.

They made it up to six claps before the pretty one dropped the ball. Amid their laughter, they were all, even the non-beauty-burdened friend, exquisite for a moment, knowing they were looked at, or maybe forgetting.

My brother and I sat, watching. His wife was pregnant at that time with their first child, a girl, and Andy was already getting too busy to play ball very often. But that night I enjoyed sitting with him, watching him watching them, appreciating girlhood for what girlhood is, as one of my connections to basketball began to fray.

Once, during my depression over Satyr, I was fooling around with this numerology book I had. The book talked about how you wrote your name down and assigned certain numbers to letters, then you added it up a certain way and divided some things into others to see what number you were.

Number one represented independence, two was the number of security, and three was the number of creativity. The book told about every number one through nine, and how they all had their strengths and weaknesses. Ones were adventurers, twos were good parents, and threes were artists. There was no good and bad, just different, everyone had his own unique contribution to make, and all the numbers had their place in the grand scheme of things.

Except for the cursed four. Fours didn't stand a snowball's chance at ever being happy for five straight minutes in a row. "Melissa" was a four. I added and divided again. Still a four. So was Melissa King, Melissa Ann King, Melissa Ann, King, Missy, and MAK.

I was going through lots of paper, wadding up and throwing away and starting over. I calculated the numbers for all the names in my immediate family, and it became obvious that I had descended from a long line of malcontents. If a scientist took a microscope and examined our DNA, he would see a bunch of grim-mouthed number fours floating around. The best my people could do was hope for a mutation.

Then I wrote down Satyr's name, my handwriting all weird and scribbly by then. I did the math. He was a three. Of *course* he was a brilliant, *interesting* three. That's the way it is when somebody dumps you: everywhere you look, you see that there was a damn good reason for it. *You* would break up with you.

But second by second, you get over it, and eventually someone better or worse comes around, and finally you're able to say maybe there was or maybe there wasn't a damn good reason for it, and maybe that's just the way it is.

His name is Bill. We met in a bar. I was there with some of the people from the new good marketing job I had, and he looked over at me from another table and waved, all friendly and quirky-moving and putting himself out there a little. He approached, and we talked, and when we danced, he didn't feel like a stranger, and at the end of the night, he didn't get all creepy and try to work his way over to my house, acting like we were on the sinking *Titanic* or something.

Bill didn't keep his answering machine volume turned down,

or make a policy of not answering his phone when I was at his house, or ask me out for Wednesday night but not Saturday, or start lots of stories with "a friend of mine" and you know "friend" is a euphemism for former-girlfriend-I-will-sleep-with-again-the-first-chance-I-get. In my thirties, that kind of stuff was beginning to mean quite a lot. It *should've* meant a lot to me at twenty, or thirteen, but it takes some of us longer than others.

Bill wears glasses and he's good at math. He doesn't play basketball. It makes him nervous, so he doesn't do it. I guess opposites attract.

One time we were at Wilson Park in Fayetteville. I've never been much of a Frisbee thrower, and I like posing for accidental-looking snapshots about as much as I enjoy being carried into bedrooms like Scarlett O'Hara, so there wasn't much to occupy us.

Lying on a blanket reading a book was nice, but I was distracted by the sound of a basketball bouncing. Three guys were on the court, shooting around. I had on some reasonable sneakers, and I walked over and asked if they were trying to get a game up. By way of an answer, one of the guys turned his back to me and dribbled off, mumbling something about just shooting around. That sure made me feel like a stupid dumb-ass, in front of my new boyfriend and all, since I'd been telling him how much I played and everything.

I picked up a ball lying near the other hoop, and Bill and I shot around for a while. As I took some outside shots and he rebounded for me, I discovered my new love interest specialized in Harlem Globetrotter–style behind-the-back passes, and I jumped like a jackrabbit to catch them. After lurching for one particularly bad pass, I suggested he make an effort to land the ball somewhere in my general vicinity.

"What are you talking about?" he wanted to know. "That's the only one you've really had to jump for."

That's the way it is, for me, having a boyfriend. Half the time, I'm wondering which one of us is crazy.

After a while, a guy limping around on the sidelines asked Bill and me if one of us wanted to play. I said I did, if they were losing one, and I went over and got myself in the game.

The dude who'd snubbed me was gone, and a bunch of college guys were playing. They were sort of gorgeous, and polite, and they introduced themselves to me one by one and shook my hand. They were so homogenous-looking it was hard to remember anyone's name, except there was an Andre in there somewhere.

We organized ourselves into teams. Bill sat down on a bench and practiced spinning the ball on his finger.

As we played, I could tell all the college guys had been coached before, because they were setting screens and posting up all over the place. They were perfectly nice guys with perfect teeth and tans and hair and stomachs playing perfect fundamental basketball.

I went up for a rebound at the same time as one of the guys. We had a lot of momentum going, and we started to fall. He grabbed me by the waist, and we scrambled for a few seconds, trying not to hurt ourselves or each other. It was one of those falls that seem to go on for a long time, the kind that gives you time to fly a few inches above the ground and try to prevent yourself from getting hurt when you finally land.

I have to say, that combination of waist grabbing, protectiveness, speed, and the right moves while time stood still was darned attractive on a pretty boy. Almost nothing sexy ever happens on the basketball court, but if something sexy *is* going to happen, it'll be when your boyfriend is watching, guaranteed.

When the college guy and I came to a stop, we had nothing but our fingers and toes on the ground. We froze for a second before working ourselves out of a position straight from the Twister game book.

The ball rolled out of bounds, and the guy ran after it. I hopped up, dusted off my hands, and smiled to show I was okay, then glanced over at Bill on the bench. He grinned and gave me a little wave.

After the game, the well-kept dudes left, and I sat down on the bench by Bill.

The next players were a mix of goof-off geeks and fraternity dudes who played basketball the way they might do anything else, dabbling in the game just for something to do. A few of them played well, but their attitudes weren't particularly ominous.

Three black guys wandered up, ready to play as a team. They were relaxed, smiling, joking around, and the white team looked suddenly nervous. To make their four, the black guys picked up a spacy-looking white kid standing on the sidelines. "It's you and the black guys," one guy said to the spacy kid, so he could remember who was on his team. Everyone laughed a little, and they started to play.

The white team's best player was tall and clean-cut, with Greek letters on his T-shirt. He played serious but under control, and he never got mad or flustered, or even tired, because he didn't waste his energy trying to steal every pass or running hard on fast breaks when he had no chance of getting down to the other end before the shot. The guy could dunk, and he would sometimes, quietly deflating everyone on the other team when he did it.

The leader of the black guys had a talent for trash talk the likes of which I've never seen before or since. He worked off the white team's tense faces, his easy confidence more daunting than the good guy's dunks. He missed a lot of shots, but he acted shocked at every brick, and he kept up a running commentary on everyone's playing. "He saw the light, and the light looked like some money to him!" he'd yell, or, "That's illegal, pimp!"

The players on the white team laughed at all the wild stuff the Trash Talker said, except for the Dunker, who appeared to ignore him. The Talker's teammates kept slight smiles on their faces and said little.

From the point guard position, Trash Talker had a good view of all the players, and he began to home in on Dunker, directing his mouth at him in a way that made you almost forget anyone out there except the two of them. Before long, Talker had noticed the one thing Dunker was bad at, and he started going on at Dunker's man, saying, "Make him put the ball on the ground! He can't dribble!"

Talker could have been a politician, with his gifts for assessment and ruthlessness. On the face of it, he was motivating his teammate, but the only person he was really talking to was Dunker, and after a good bit of "he can't dribble" Dunker changed from doing what he did well—every single thing except dribble—to focusing on what he couldn't do. He began to bounce the ball randomly out on the wing, slowing the game and tiring all his teammates out as they tried to keep moving and stay open.

Trash Talker was visibly stimulated by the sight of the weakening Dunker, like some kind of jackal perceiving an antelope's first stumble.

"Look! All he's doing is dribbling around in circles! That's all he's doing!" the Talker kept yelling. He sounded hungry, anxious to set someone up and see him fall. It would have seemed impossible a half-hour earlier, but the Dunker began to look awkward and exposed, dribbling around in circles like he was under a spell.

It took another three or four plays for the Dunker to remember he was the best player out there. He swished a nice outside basket, and then, on defense, he blocked a shot. Talker's juju was broken, but it had worked long enough for Dunker's team to get behind, and they lost.

I looked over at Bill and thought of him punching his answering machine button because it wouldn't occur to him to do otherwise. Whether it's love or basketball or most anything, I guess some people play the game, and some people play the game outside the game. Trash talk is everywhere. Some people, like the rawboned dude working the desk at Jones, are cocky and campy with it, like a child doing a trick to get your attention and make friends with you. They're the best. Or someone can be dishonest and political and reasonable-toned with their "when I say *nigger* I don't mean *black*" trash. Or they can be fake-accidental, using it to hunt, sneaky and waiting for their chance, like my sheepish mugger way back in Chicago, or the Ringleader who didn't know what the score was. The politicians and the hunters act like they're calling it like they see it, but they really hope you'll see it like they call it.

Sitting on that bench with Bill, it seemed like guilelessness could be the most important thing in the world.

I'm not big or talented, but I've always been quick and had good endurance. My defensive strategy is to wear people out as much as stop them, and I get my share of steals.

One day I lunged to pick off a pass, and I discovered something strange had happened. Just like that, I'd lost a step. I was a touch slower, but I could still feel that missing first move in the moment it should have been there, shadowy and present and vaguely amputated. You'd think something like that would happen so gradually you wouldn't notice it. You'd think the player inside wouldn't fall away in discernible pieces like chunks of a bad tooth.

When a thirteen-year-old happily hollered "Pass it to the lady!" a couple more chunks fell away.

A few weeks later, I was watching a WNBA game, and I noticed that one of the players looked older than all the others. I jumped up and got on my computer to find the WNBA website, and I learned the player was thirty-five, just like me. I scanned all the other teams' information to see if anyone was older than that. No one was.

Thoughts about looking like someone's mother diminished the fortitude I needed to get myself in games. I started to become more particular about situations, anxious to avoid any further falling away.

I'm not sure whether it was coincidence or not, but at the same time I was becoming more preoccupied with Bill the guileless boyfriend, an affable, movie-watching, Scrabble-playing, dinner-eating fixture in my house. Then, one Saturday morning, I asked Bill would he please vacuum while I went to the store for groceries.

"Vacuum what?" he wanted to know.

I went to the closet, got my ball, and headed for the Springdale Youth Center, leaving Bill to eat mustard sandwiches and ponder the subterranean meanings of the word *vacuum*.

I'd never played at the Youth Center, but I'd heard about games there on the weekends. I felt kind of jittery about going there, because it was a new place and I hadn't played in a while, but when I arrived, I was relieved to see plenty of older guys and a few casual adolescents forming a ragtag group my fat and happy butt had half a chance of keeping up with.

We were about to start a game when a guy made a joke about playing shirts and skins, pointing to me and saying, "You're on skins." Believe me, I've heard *that* one before, but I laughed a little anyway.

I was guarding a Hispanic guy carrying thirty extra pounds. He was surprisingly agile, which made me think he hadn't always been overweight. Like a blind person who could once see, he had the competence of someone with a reference point to a former self.

On a fast break, he and I stood and watched everyone speed off, giving each other an excuse to loaf.

"I'm thirty-seven," he said, "so I'm lucky I can play at all. It's my knees. They kill me."

He patted his big belly to indicate it was to blame. Then he hesitated for a second before seeming to decide I wouldn't mind if he asked how old I was.

When I told him I was thirty-five, there was some new respect on his face when he said, "Well, you're doin' all right then."

When someone's surprised that you're as old as you are, are you supposed to be glad, or not? I still haven't figured that one out.

I went to the Youth Center again on a weeknight and found a group of postcollege corporate-looking in-shape definitely not ragtag guys. I almost walked back out, and I should have, in my insecure frame of mind and with my out-of-shape body, but I went ahead and played, badly.

After the game, I was headed for the water fountain when a good-looking guy who had been on my team walked past me, made eye contact, and looked away quickly, which I interpreted as an invitation to go ahead and not come back. Usually people say good game, or at least nod, after you play with them. I've been snubbed plenty trying to get *in* games, but damn, that was a new kind of lonely, being snubbed afterward.

My brother and the rest of the world were moving on. Pro players my age were dinosaurs. *Pass it to the lady.* Everywhere I looked, the signs were there. The game was packing its bags, and maybe not today, and maybe not tomorrow, but soon, it would be leaving me behind. It was inevitable, really. Being a gym rat is great and everything, but there's just no future in it.

Training Camp

THE IMAGE of myself as some future crazy dribbling granny wasn't strictly thrilling, but what was going to take the place of basketball? Toenail painting? Pilates? Pampered Chef parties?

Maybe I still had enough game to keep going for a few more years. Maybe all I needed was a little extra training. Maybe I wasn't exactly what you'd call well rounded, but be that as it may, I wasn't ready to hang up my high-tops.

I saw an article in a magazine about a basketball camp for adults, and I got their brochure. "Maybe you're new to the game," it said, "or maybe you never got a fair chance in high school. Maybe you want to recapture the feeling of clarity and self control in the face of stiff competition, the confidence and presence of mind to know when to shoot and when to pass. Maybe you want to get back to something you haven't felt in a while. Maybe you want to play forever."

The Never Too Late basketball camp was in the maybe business, and I was buying. "It'll be a little vacation," I said to my coworkers, hoping to come across as a hip adult adventure type person and not desperate as a middle-aged wife clamoring to get the attention of her husband.

"Probably gonna be a lot of lesbians there," one of the coworkers said.

This nugget of wisdom reminded me of a guy years earlier who had informed me, when I was moving to Chicago, that there were "lots of blacks there." Out of all the comments someone might have made about Chicago, like "Try not to freeze to death," "Go Cubs," or even just "Good luck," that's what he said, "lots of blacks."

Then he looked me in the eyes for a few seconds, all intense, dying to hear me say yeah, I hate those bastards.

I arrived at the Racebrook Lodge in Sheffield, Massachusetts, at the same time as Toni and Helen, who had driven in from Manhattan. Toni was a stocky, talkative girl wearing a baseball cap and knee-length denim shorts. Helen wore big, dark sunglasses and remained silent, opting to express herself through her tie-dyed T-shirt with antelope-like creatures performing a drumming ritual all over it. Helen wasn't there to play but had come along to meditate by the river, Toni told me.

I went to my room and emptied my bag of gym shorts and socks and T-shirts into a dresser drawer. It was too early to go to the initial camp meeting in the dining room, but as soon as I sat down on the edge of one of the beds to wait, I felt a sudden dread of an imminent unpacking stranger. So I got the hell out of lodge and hiked to the waterfall that was promised at the top of the stream running along the Racebrook grounds. When I made it back to the dining room, thirteen women had gathered around a farm table. At least thirty years of age separated the youngest from the oldest. I was somewhere in the middle.

The owner and coach of Never Too Late, Steve, was a short, extremely fit, clean-cut white guy in his late forties. He opened our meeting by asking us to go around the table telling what our name was, where we were from, and what we did for a living. The other coach, Leslie, a thirtyish black woman employed only for the women's camp, added she'd like to hear about our favorite basketball memory.

One by one, we admitted things about being grown adult women who couldn't help it, we just loved to play basketball. We listened to each other's stories about trying to get in with the guys, not being passed the ball, hovering on sidelines. We laughed generously when someone made a joke, nodding and commiserating at every revealed vulnerability, like we were making our public confessions at a twelve-step program.

During the forty-five minutes it took us to make it around the table, Steve looked at his watch a number of times, but he seemed hesitant to interrupt.

"This is pretty different than the men's camp," Steve said with a chuckle when we finally finished sharing. He started mumbling and shrugging oafishly, imitating the male campers' spartan self-introduction. "Urrr, hi, yeah, I'm Jim from Brooklyn. I'm in banking. When do we scrimmage?"

He looked at the woman sitting next to him as if to turn the floor over to her. Everyone laughed at the caricature, except Toni, who squinted at Steve like she was drawing a conclusion about him.

Steve wrapped up the meeting and then took off jogging the mile or so over to the high school gym where we'd be playing. By the time we campers figured out who was going with whom and giggled our way into various cars and drove over, Steve was waiting on us.

He promptly got down to business, asking us to form two lines for a continuous drill that had us start at half-court, dribble up to the lane, then take two steps and shoot a lay-up. As our right foot hit the edge of the lane, we were supposed to make sure the ball bounced while our left foot was down, then take one more step and lay it up. Steve had Leslie demonstrate, and she made it look as though nothing could be easier.

And nothing could have been easier, but when it was my turn, I started thinking about where every step and bounce was supposed to happen, and I kept getting all tangled up. I'd take off dribbling from half-court, get to the edge of the lane, stutter-step trying to coordinate my feet and the ball, pick up my dribble, commit a serious traveling violation, and then throw the ball in the general direction of the hoop.

It was like I'd never held a basketball in my hands, and with a whole weekend of high-quality basketball instruction in front of me, I felt a low-level panic that only got worse when Leslie or Steve started giving me pointers. Thinking about *how* to do something I did all the time, I couldn't do it. Most of the other campers weren't faring any better.

· · ·

Okay, here it is: I was a high school benchwarmer. There's more. Every team I was on sucked.

The only playing time I got was in the fourth quarter when we were at least twenty points behind. During games, I kept one desperate eye on the score clock, hoping we'd win, but that if we *were* going to lose, we'd lose big, so I could get in. I got the second version of my wish most every game with about five minutes left, when Coach would look at the clock, heave that dejected sigh all the benchwarmers had been waiting for, and wave us angrily into the game. We'd tear off our warm-up jerseys and scramble over each other to go crouch en masse at the scorekeeper's bench, watching precious seconds disappear until a foul was called or someone went out of bounds. Then the ref would point at us, and we were in, giddy stowaways on a ship headed straight for Loserville.

Some of us remembered the plays from practice, but most of us didn't. Either way it didn't matter, because we all shot every time we got our hands on the ball in frantic attempts to make U-turns in our heretofore sad athletic journeys. Unlike practice, a game had *witnesses.* If we could only score, or make a steal, or block a shot, maybe Coach would have to play us next time when the crowd chanted our names and the parents initiated letter-writing campaigns.

But the U-turns never happened. There were probably some very good reasons we weren't getting more playing time than we were, and besides, it's hard to make a real name for yourself in three minutes of pandemonium.

My fiasco of a high school basketball career started in eighth grade, with Coach Danner. He was new that year, and the first time we ever saw him, he introduced himself to all of us trying out for the team by saying that most people thought he looked like Burt Reynolds. Except for being a little chubby, Coach actually did look like Burt Reynolds, because he had black hair, a thick mustache, chest hairs poking out from the collar of his polo shirt, and white teeth sparkling against a perpetual tan.

Coach Danner promptly chose a pet, a preacher's daughter named Kimmy Jamison who resembled a younger and happier version of Coach's wife. Kimmy was as plump and short and creamy-skinned as a baby, and she was *going* to be Coach's star. The problem was where to put her. At five-foot-two, she obviously wasn't a post player. She also wasn't quick or a good ball handler or authoritative on the floor, so she wasn't point guard material either. She could usually catch a pass, though, and Coach talked a lot about what a beautiful shot she had, so he made her one of his starting forwards.

I was five-foot-five and ninety-five pounds, and commonly referred to as a "beanpole." Unlike Kimmy, I did not belong draped and lounging on a velvet couch. I was freckled and all braces and legs.

All the girls on the team clamored to get near Coach, but the starters had propriety over him during walks back and forth between the school and gym, or on bus trips, or in the bleachers while the boys played their games. They rushed by the rest of us to get to him, and we benchwarmers knew it wasn't our place to do anything other than let them go by.

There was a song we used to sing to Coach when he came down to our dressing room just before we were ready to go out for a game.

> *We love you, Coach,*
> *Oh yes, we do.*
> *We love you, Coach,*
> *It's true.*
> *When you're not with us,*
> *We're blue!*
> *Oh Coach Danner, we love you!*

I swear, we really did sing that piece of crap to him, clapping our hands real peppy the whole time. Mostly we sang the song when we felt guilty because we were losing so much and he seemed depressed.

Unlike the more athletic players with short hair and muscular legs, Kimmy never had to work to get Coach's attention. He just found his way to her. During practice, Coach would sometimes take Kimmy aside to talk to her while the rest of us ran drills. Once, I looked over to the side of the court to see him lying down on his side, his head propped up on his arm, like Burt's *Playgirl* centerfold pose. He gazed up at Kimmy, who was seated Indian-style on the floor, all good posture and charm. This went on until the whole team was furious, every single one of us a sweaty woman scorned.

One day we were scrimmaging, the A team against the B team, as usual. I blocked two of Kimmy's shots, and Coach Danner stopped practice and told her to throw the basketball at my face next time, and that would put a stop to me blocking her shots. He looked at me when he said it to her.

Kimmy never hit me with the ball, though. You just don't hit a girl wearing braces in the face with a basketball at point-blank range unless you're a mean person, which she wasn't.

Coach and Kimmy made me think about those couples you see in public sometimes, the man all unlikable and bitching at some powerless clerk or waitress, the woman with a sad, vacant look on her face. She knows he's a good person, way underneath, but she can't understand the things he does sometimes.

We were paired off running hundred-yard dashes one day in the off-season, and I was racing Kimmy. She wasn't very fast, and I beat her every time. Coach was getting mad, and he told the team we would have to stay out there and keep running until Kimmy won a race. That was just fine with me; I would've dropped dead of a heart attack before I let her win. It was personal, not between me and Kimmy, but between me and Coach. So I just kept running harder, and Kimmy ran harder, too, moving her short legs as fast as she could, like a pampered horse confused about why she was being pushed so hard all of a sudden.

In a foot race, long-legged and pissed-off beats plump and obedient every time. Coach finally gave up and told us to go in. He might have been more hardheaded about it, but it was pretty stupid of him to say we would stay until Kimmy won. Our practice was scheduled for one hour during the school day, and he really couldn't keep the entire basketball team outside all afternoon to act out his dramas while we missed social studies class.

Eventually, Coach Danner started flirting with a married secretary at the school. She was the one who took the lunch money from everybody in the cafeteria, and she had gleaming white teeth, too. I can still remember how they used to grin at each other, Coach Danner ducking his head and looking at the floor in his impression of boyish charm, her looking up at his face from her chair and her money tray. They were pretty obvious about it.

Then one day Coach was gone, didn't even finish out the school year. Kimmy quit the team and became a cheerleader.

That was Kimmy. As for me, after Coach Danner left, we got a new coach, but I still never started at basketball, still never got in unless our still very bad teams were at least twenty points behind. The new coach got me focused on running track, and I was good at that, but even though I liked getting my name in the paper and collecting the trophies, the act of running itself didn't mean that much to me.

Now, on the other side of a couple of decades, I like to hope that a transformation happened. I like to hope that gangly awkwardness has morphed into something that doesn't give me away as such an easy touch, that I can walk through cesspools like Coach Danner's with some wading boots on. I think the truth is sometimes I do, and sometimes I collect more trash than the garbage man.

There's a dream I've been having off and on for a few years now. I'm running the two-mile, my strongest race, in a high school track meet. People are watching from the bleachers. I'm ahead, running easily, feeling like I'll never have to slow down, but after a few laps, everything starts to feel heavy. It's like the air, the entire atmosphere, is pushing all its weight down on me. I feel my body begin to yield to the pressure, and I gradually fall forward, until finally I have no choice but to use my knuckles to skip along the ground like a monkey, still struggling to keep up, not having much of a chance, obviously, against all the bipeds.

Don't ask me what the hell it all means. But it's pretty different from that weightless basketball dream I told you about, the one where I'm flying through the air and no one can stop me.

I guess running was like an uncomplicated, predictable man, the one who makes you feel oppressed by his always being there, doing the right thing, the one you take for granted. Basketball is the Tricky Dick, the guy who always knows what to say and is never where he's supposed to be, the half-willing one always disappearing, leaving you too soon and with something to think about, pining for the next time. I've never gotten over basketball.

After practice, Leslie, Rhonda, Lynn, and I went for pizza. Rhonda was in her thirties, a native New Yorker working as a social worker in Boston, and Lynn was a fifty-five-year-old nurse from Connecticut who had recently gotten a law degree.

Leslie had either played or coached basketball her whole life, and she was successful, too: her high school girls' team had just won the state championship. She told funny stories, she was articulate and friendly, and when you talked to her, she looked at you like she was really paying attention.

The nurse and the social worker fell easily into conversation.

"You're with a needle exchange program?" Lynn asked Rhonda. "Are you allowed to serve minors?"

Rhonda said no, she didn't work with kids, and she discussed some of the reasons for a while.

I could feel the floor being handed over to me.

"How long have you been doing that work?" I asked Rhonda.

She told us, and when the next pause came, Leslie, chewing, jumped as if she'd been called on in class.

"So, Rhonda," Leslie said, "you find that you don't work with kids very much then?"

If the substance wasn't there, the professional demeanor was. Leslie nailed the courteous and interested tone of voice, the facial expression, the handling of her fork. Something about her talent for quick study made me suspect she found it a little unfathomable, watching all us attorneys and nurses and social workers and copy writers pay $450 for three days' worth of bouncing balls off our toes and saying, "Wait, now, tell me again, which foot goes first?"

At practice, when Steve said, "Show 'em, Leslie," she would dribble backwards and forwards, her head up, her body leaning over slightly, her nondribbling arm in front of her protecting the ball, bouncing low and snappy, natural as jumping to a grass-hopper as Steve would shout, "Yes! Now that's what ball handling looks like!"

Hearing Steve tell us all about how dribbling is supposed to *look* made me think about how, when you're playing pickup ball and don't have refs, everyone knows when somebody travels. When it happens, the players on the other team say, "Whoa!" and "All right now," or they slap themselves on the forehead like they can't believe it, letting everyone know they saw the walk. A really honest, serious type of player—someone like ol' Fair Guy at Reed Park back in Santa Monica—might stop in mid-drive and throw the ball off to the side before anyone can say anything, because he felt himself carry it even before everyone else saw. He knows what traveling *feels* like.

Sometimes you can't say exactly what the traveler did with his feet and hands and the ball. The violation may be obvious, but sometimes it's a matter of effect, and you only know it looked like a travel, so it was. To be good at basketball, you have to see, and do, the whole without necessarily understanding all the parts. Maybe the great players can operate on both levels.

Steve had also told us how confidence looks. "Don't stand over there waiting to get in a game looking like this," he said, dribbling high and out of control, like the ball was a dog pulling him along by the leash. Watching him, it seemed unlikely, in one and a half days, that we would get around to all that Zen stuff the brochure talked about.

Lynn recalled the days when she played high school ball. Back then, girls played half-court with six players, three guards on one end and three forwards on the other, because they were considered too delicate to run up and down the court.

Lynn said she'd cried when she watched the first WNBA game. Then she told us about how she went with a friend her age to shoot baskets sometimes. Two little boys had approached them recently, sized them up, then challenged them to two-on-two. When Lynn told about it, you could tell she'd been a little honored to be asked, like a real player.

That night, when I went back to my room, I found my roommate, Gloria, in one of the beds, awake and taking notes about the night's practice in a little memo pad. She stopped writing to talk, and within a few minutes, I'd learned that Gloria was a forty-year-old photographer from Boston who lived with her partner, Lucy.

Gloria was polite, soft-spoken, and earnest. She struck me as intellectual, with her note taking and horn-rimmed glasses and tight smile.

Something about being alone in a room with Gloria's methodical East Coast lesbian mildness transformed me into the wild-eyed southern overly heterosexual loudmouth I'm usually not. I don't know what got into me, but I started acting like this girl my brother used to date, a squeaky well-intentioned arm-ornament who smelled like perfume and new clothes every day. The girlfriend always arrived at my mother's house with an enthusiastic greeting of the dog. She'd shriek, "*HI LITTLE BABY SWEET GIRL HOW ARE YOUUUUU BOO BOO BOO BOO!?*" her voice so high it sounded like she'd been freebasing helium and speed. My mom's spitz, having spent the day alternately dozing and staring at the front door waiting for it to open, said hello to the girlfriend by peeing on the floor in excitement, every time. Mom would always say, "Don't *talk* to her like that!" but the girlfriend couldn't help it. She'd just forget and do it again the next time.

In college, I thought of some sorority girls as the kind that made dogs pee. A group of them would see another group of them going to class, and they would block the sidewalk and stop everyone else from walking while they caught up after not having seen each other for the last fifteen minutes, screaming, "*HEYYYY HOW ARE Y'ALL OH MY GOD LOOK AT YOU YOU'RE SO TAN IS THAT A NEW BACKPACK?!*" and I always thought about what if they just peed right there on the sidewalk.

All poor Gloria wanted to do was write in her memo pad, and I burst into her space with all my having so much fun and everyone being so nice and I just couldn't wait until tomorrow. She was too polite to do anything other than give a half-smile and nod, but she never really put her pencil down.

At six-thirty the next morning, I went down to breakfast. One other camper, Floris, was up and getting breakfast, too. Floris was a fifty-year-old black woman with a short tasteful natural and beautiful hands. She hadn't played much basketball, and she'd told us during our first meeting how she'd been watching a group of young women play back home in D.C. They were fierce, she said, and she wanted to get good enough to dare going out on the court with them.

We sat down on a couch together. The quiet morning room, a shushing cook who kept reminding everyone not to wake the guests sleeping upstairs, and the fleeting nature of the weekend made the situation ripe for confidences, and we soon fell into a discussion about men. Her theories were based on empirical evidence gathered from a subject named Harold, while my own findings were more generalized, but our dialogue was well balanced and informed.

"Thoughtless!" she spat.

"Selfish!" I hissed, after careful consideration.

"Stupid! Dumb stuff that made me just look at him and say, 'Have you *lost* your fool *mind*?' And oh my lord, he was such a whiner. This was a man who had been in and out of prison. Six-foot-three and two hundred and fifty pounds. Got scars all over his body. And he would always be saying, 'Angel . . .' (that's what he called me, Angel) . . . 'Angel, baby, my back hurts.'"

She drew out the words, squinted her eyes, and wrinkled her nose in an elaborate nasal whine.

"Yeah, that's just how he talked," she continued, building steam. "'Aaaangel, my baaaack hurts.' So I bought him some of that Heet. You know, H-E-E-T, Heet? And I put some of that on him. Now, he just had scars all up and down his body" (Floris moved her hand lightly along her shoulder and arm and looked away from me, as if she had recaptured for a moment the feeling of touching him). "This big tough guy, right? Well, I put that Heet on him, and all he could say was, 'Owwww! That buuuuurnnnns!'"

I snorted, rolled my eyes.

"So then I started saying to him all the time, 'Honey, can I rub your back?' or, 'Do you want an aspirin?' or, 'Should I make you a doctor's appointment?' and he'd say, 'Nooooo, nooooo, Angel, that's okay.'"

She breathed what was evidently one of the man's long, woeful sighs.

"Finally, I learned just to go into my Stepford Wife mode, and when he'd start whining about his back, I'd say, 'Honey, would you like a glass of wine?' And he'd say yes, that would be nice, and I don't know what the wine had to do with his back, but he'd quit his bitchin' then."

I conjured up a memory of some boyfriend or another. It was fuel. "God!" I said. "It's like you have to shut off a part of your *brain* to deal with them! It's like, how old are you, five? What am I, your mother? And you know what else? I'm sick of all this 'make him a better man' crap. It's . . . it's like . . ."

I paused, searching for the right word to express the nuance of my feelings.

"Stupid!"

Harold the 250-pound wimp had died a year earlier, in the passenger's seat of Floris's car. Since the accident, Floris had been busy putting the slip on a bad case of survivor's guilt by running marathons, taking belly dancing classes, planning a trip to Brazil, and attending basketball camps.

Floris had a way of turning every subject back to Harold, or the accident.

"It was a Friday afternoon," she said from out of nowhere, her voice soft and distant, "just a Friday afternoon, and we were having a conversation, you know, about not much of anything. We weren't battling, thank God, and then it happened, it just happened, and I couldn't do anything but sit there and watch him go."

Most of the time I get uncomfortable when someone starts crying. The worst is when people are interviewed on television, standing in front of their burnt-down house or talking about somebody dying. I feel sorry for them, but more often than not, when I see people crying, it feels dramatic, not real, as if they're not sure they feel the way they think they're supposed to, with everybody watching. Floris wasn't like that. Her tears just came, and she wiped them off her face with the palm of her hand and kept talking, casual and thoughtless as waving off a fly.

The other campers were beginning to stream in for breakfast, and as the first-thing-in-the-morning sounds of plates and silverware and groggy conversation filtered in, Floris suddenly started giving me advice, like she needed to and had to hurry.

"Well," she said, "if you can find one that's half-decent, and if there's a little passion, and if he loves you, you might as well hang on to him, because they're all going to drive you crazy anyway."

"So give up on finding a mature adult?"

"Oh please, yes, forget *all* about that."

Floris's eyes got liquidy again when she laughed, and she seemed so fragile and determined it was a little hard to look at her.

"The thing about Harold was, he loved me. One time he said to me, 'Angel, you're so beautiful, why don't you dress yourself up more?' He wanted me to wear some of these ridiculous white hot pants he saw. I looked at him and thought, *Anybody crazy enough to want to see my old ass in a pair of hot pants deserves to be loved.* That man, he loved me."

● ● ●

Never Too Late provided the services of a coach-EMT who led us in stretching exercises and then stood on the sidelines all day, ready to spring into action at the first hint of injury or heart attack. In lieu of any such emergencies, stretching was the most active part of the EMT's day, and he took this job seriously.

After thirty-five minutes of contorting ourselves into various positions, we were lying on our backs with our right feet pulled over our heads when Steve hollered, "At the guys' camp, this is the point where I usually made a joke about the Kamasutra! But I'm not gonna say it this time!"

Toni issued a disapproving snort while the rest of us giggled.

We began our day with shooting. Steve gave us all kinds of tips about our feet, our eyes, our elbows, our fingers, and then he told us to choose one of his tips and concentrate only on that one thing as we shot around in pairs. He went around to everyone on the court, quietly asking each of us, "What are you thinking about?"

When he got to Rhonda, the social worker from New York, she said, "Making the shot!" Steve's jaw clenched a little at her attempt to be cute. Trying to make the shot was exactly what we *weren't* supposed to be thinking about.

Then we started in on the star drill, which high school teams often use to warm up in front of the crowd before games. Leslie and Steve began by showing us how to do the convoluted thing as we stood on the sidelines with "oh shit" looks on our faces. After they demonstrated, we got going, having not much of a choice other than to give it a try. We screwed up like crazy at first, but the weird thing was, before we knew it, we were doing it right, moving in and out of four different lines and passing several basketballs to the people we were supposed to. From above, we must have looked like a well-disciplined team, and we didn't even know how we were doing it, which I guess was the point.

Floris got hit upside the head with the ball and passed to the wrong person and got in the wrong lines until she dropped out, saying she needed to watch for a little while. I knew how she felt.

The same thing happened to me one time when I tried to line-dance at a country western bar. I kept bumping into people and messing everyone up, and once that starts happening, believe me, you can't think about anything other than getting the hell off the floor.

Floris never jumped back into the star drill. She just stood by herself as the rest of us reveled in doing something we thought we couldn't. After it was over, we broke for lunch, and Steve told us to eat well, because when we came back, we'd be working on the motion offense, "a good little play for leagues or pickup games." He took off running and beat us back to the lodge.

The motion offense drill works like this. One girl starts with the ball, and her two nearest teammates screen away on another teammate's defender. Then the girl with the ball passes, and the drill repeats from the new position.

It sounds simple enough, but it was even more confusing than the star drill. I used to do it a million years ago in high school, so I remembered the basics. Floris didn't even attempt this one, and I worried about her a little as she watched from the sidelines. I was afraid that, standing over there by herself, she'd start wondering what the hell she was doing at the camp, and her life would catch up with her. It wasn't like I thought she *should* be wondering that, but I knew I would have.

Shannon, a thirty-nine-year-old cross trainer from Connecticut, was a defender in the drill, and she kept stealing passes, even though the defense was supposed to be there just for position. Steve would say, "Let's not steal the passes right now and just let them get used to the offense okay please," and then the ball would go around a few times and Shannon would just forget and steal it again, like some crazy thoroughbred race dog who won't stop chasing the rabbit.

Later, when Shannon was on offense, she had no idea where to go, and I noticed Steve's jaw clench again as he reexplained the drill to her.

Finally, it was time to scrimmage. We were supposed to incorporate everything we'd learned that day into our game, but when I got out there, I acted sort of like Shannon. I forgot about the motion offense and started running around all over the place, not setting screens and not posting up.

The only thing I'd recaptured was the feeling of pandemonium, and it hit me that I needed to stop being so hell-bent on doing my own thing every minute, trying to earn respect by sweating more than anyone else, by being different. This time, unlike the lay-up drill, I didn't fall into being my fifteen-year-old self. Instead, I saw her running around all skinny and pell-mell, making Coach Danner's jaw clench. Sure, he was a colossal a-hole, but from this new vantage point, it looked like my game and my life had been burdened by too many accidental rebellions I had no chance of winning.

That night, we campers went out to dinner at a nice restaurant in town. I sat by Floris, and she told us all about her recent Internet dates, how she'd ditched one guy for being sappy and sending her flowers after their first encounter. If she was that finicky, I wondered, how did Harold the hypochondriac ex-con wino ever get in with her? I suspected it must have involved some lying.

Lana sat across the table from me. She was a super-fit fifty-year-old with three teenage girls. The more wine she drank, the more she talked about leaving her husband ten years earlier, and how she regretted it, even though he'd been cheating on her and she couldn't stand him.

"It's been so hard," she said. Then she looked at me, the single, younger but about-to-be-too-old-for-choices one across the table, and again I got the feeling of urgent advice being thrown to me.

"It doesn't matter where they put that *thing*, so just don't even think about it," she said.

I was taken aback by the disgust in her voice, but that didn't prevent me from wondering if she was right.

Toni had skipped dinner, and I wondered if Steve was a little relieved, with her talent for sniffing out differences between our camp and the mens'.

For a couple of hours we drank too much and talked too loud, we had trouble with the pepper mill, we ordered dessert, and by the time our waitress started dropping hints that it was time to go, the oldest camper was snoozing on one side of me, and Floris was staring sadly at her coffee cup on the other. Had we been at the restaurant as mothers or wives or professionals, I'm sure we'd have been quite civilized, but we were on reprieve from adulthood, with all its guilt and disappointment, even as the oldest among us said so urgently, *Settle, settle, settle . . . settle for what's not hard and never burden yourself with the foolishness that it's all supposed to mean something.*

The last day of camp ended at noon, and after practice, Steve had us gather around in a circle to hear his final comments on being pickup-worthy.

"You gotta look like a player when you're out there trying to get in. Take a few shots, dribble around with authority. Don't go in there like this," he said, taking off and shooting a lay-up in a herky-jerky leg-kicking push-the-ball sort of way that was the counterpart of throwing like a girl, "or nobody'll pick you."

Then Steve had us get in a circle, look at the person next to us, and think of one positive thing about that person's game, and one thing that person needed to work on.

"Do you do this at the guys' camp?!"

Steve looked at Toni and said, actually, uh, no, he didn't, but he thought he might give it a try here with us.

She heaved a disgusted sigh.

Floris complimented Shannon for being aggressive and getting all those steals during the motion offense drill. A lot of the weekend had been lost on her, I guessed, but I hoped the fierce women back in D.C., knowing nothing of her traumas, would let her in anyway.

Then we all scattered back to our lives as grown adult women yearning to move and play as well as we could, each of us deciding between resignation and saying no to our own brand of what didn't feel like living, each of us dealing with what was and wasn't too late, each of us hoping the game we loved would love us back, at least every now and then.

Sidelines

TRUTH WAS, in my mid-thirties, it really was getting too late to be hovering around the court, looking for a game with teenage boys. It wasn't that I was more likely get hurt, or that I couldn't play, or that I didn't enjoy the game, but that I might get laughed at or ignored. It wasn't that I had less courage, but that so much more of it was being required.

I was only beginning to notice my brain's growing collection of basketball memories kept, filed, accessed, learned from, guessed about, and mythologized. Without realizing it, on the courts and in the parks surrounding them, I'd been searching for clues to the mystery of how to live.

Like this college-age girl I saw one time helping a little kid learn how to play. She was in the lane, teaching the kid about defense and ball handling, encouraging him to shoot and telling him how great he was doing. The college girl wore cute basketball clothes, with current sweats and a crop top, and she looked appealing. She wasn't glancing at the door or the clock every two minutes; she was content to be doing what she was doing. She looked like a player, too, someone who could hang, someone who might get in a game after a while, but it was okay if she didn't, too. You just knew that girl deflected shit like Teflon.

This was the life fantasy that pulled me toward a preliminary phone call to find out about coaching at the local Boys and Girls Club. I was put right through to the volunteer coordinator.

"You played some?" he asked me.

"Well, yes," I said, "in high school, and I still play pickup ball when I get the chance, but I don't have any coaching background, or even much experience with—"

"You'll be fine. There's not much to know, really, at this level. How about fourth-grade girls?"

Before I got off the phone, I was a coach, and a few weeks later, I was at a coaches' meeting, notepad and pencil in hand, ready to jot down tips on preferred offenses for ten-year-olds. But no hints or structure or philosophy were provided; we simply picked up our list of players, game schedule, and practice times and signed an agreement that we wouldn't cuss or otherwise be bad examples. Then we were dismissed.

I'm not sure what I expected, but I left in some mental distress, with my first practice in two days. On the way home, I stopped by the bookstore and bought a copy of *Great Basketball Drills for Baffled Parents*. Later that night, settling into bed with *Baffled* and a highlighter, I began to wonder what the hell I was thinking, trying to be a coach, a contributing member of the community and everything, a *grown-up*. I didn't have much experience with any of that.

I called all the girls' parents on the phone before our practice, and through these conversations I discovered that there were a surprising number of "gifted little athletes" on my team. That was good, I thought, the more GLAs the better.

I also spent an embarrassing amount of time putting together my coaching look. I didn't want to dress too much like the girls, and I didn't want to look like their moms. The most successful lady coaches I'd ever paid any attention to were Pat Summitt of the UT Volunteers, prancing around in front of the bench with her business suits and high heels on, and Coach MacRae, the only lady coach we faced in my high school district. Coach MacRae had worn the same polyester Russell gear as the men coaches. She had a gray crew cut and won a lot of games, and many citizens said she was a "morphodite." They said that was fine and all, but why did she have to run the score up on everybody?

I finally threw on Gap sweatpants and a T-shirt and placed around my neck the shiny new whistle that Bill the boyfriend had bought me for the occasion. He'd even had it engraved with the year and my initials. As I walked into the gym wearing my whistle and carrying a notebook with my practice outline, I may have vaguely resembled a coach, but what I felt like was a poser.

I had come an hour early to spy on some other practices. Two teams were there, using the side goals. The first team had ten players and three coaches, and they were running drills: passing, dribbling, shooting lay-ups, and taking jump shots. They looked smooth, competent, relaxed, like a real team, and the coaches, in their slick, nylon athletic pants, looked like real coaches.

On the other side was one chubby, balding coach whose six players stood in three pairs passing balls back and forth. They were practicing at the hoop farthest away from the bleachers, where I sat listening to three mothers complain about the exorbitant price of lots in town, the maintenance on their SUVs, and all the gymnastics, tae kwon do, and piano lessons their kids had to be driven to.

One of the mothers asked me if I had a kid out there, and I told her, no, I was actually the coach of the next team, fourth-grade girls, at eight.

"Practice at eight o'clock at night?!" the woman demanded. "For fourth-graders?!"

I felt a knee-jerk guilt and mumbled something about being assigned the time.

Another of the mothers was yelling toward the court at her very short, uncoordinated, and inexperienced daughter, alternately screaming at her to relax or look at so-and-so coming in the gym.

I watched the two teams practice for a while and felt nervous, thinking about that audience of humorless parents facing another season sitting in bleachers and making dreary small talk. A jittery need to urinate was coming on, like I was about to give a presentation. I had to coach my*self*, silently repeating various twelve-step-esque codas.

I have a lot to offer these girls.

The parents will support me and appreciate my efforts.

Screw them. I'm the coach, and they can all kiss my ass.

Finally, it was time for practice. I stood under one of the hoops, fiddling with my notebook, trying to have a commanding presence, and three girls approached and stood in front of me all in a row like Siamese triplets, giggling and elbowing each other.

Emily was shy, with crooked teeth and a smile that overtook her face when you spoke to her. She was joined at the shoulder to Felicia, a dainty black girl, bright and enthusiastic, with a long, bushy ponytail that hung down her back. Rounding out this preliminary trio was surly Allison, shrugging or nodding when you asked her a question, her eyes perpetually at half-mast as if they were guarding an entrance.

A slump-shouldered tomboy arrived with her father. He quickly introduced her, making sure she was at the right place, and then he turned her over to me. "Beth!" he barked good-humoredly, "this is your coach! Listen to her! I'm going to sit up in the stands and do some work!"

She was loose, relaxed and at home in the world, and she joined the group easily.

I recognized the person who had to be Tonya. Her stepmom had told me over the phone that the girl was a GLA, tall, like her mom, who the stepmom wasn't, and that the dad was not allowed to coach Tonya's teams because he was "too serious." The stepmom and Tonya's dad made their way to the top of the bleachers carrying an infant in a car seat, sitting out of chatting range from everyone else. They wore interesting hats and black leather coats and stood out stylishly among all the rumpled parents in the gym.

And then there was Amanda. Little bitty Amanda, not even half the size of Tonya.

I memorized their names and told them mine. I said our goal was to have fun this season, that we were going to play hard and be serious, but we were gonna have fun, too. I told them to remember what I'd said, because I was going to ask them again at the end of practice, so be sure to remember our goal, which was, I reminded them, to have fun.

We started out with some drills from *Baffled*. I figured that's what the parents would want to see, lots of snappy drills, but I would have preferred to minimize the standing in line, the boredom, and all the remembering where to go on the floor and who to throw it to.

I wanted to talk to the girls about relaxing, about being in the moment and thinking on their feet, about not being married to outcomes, about that stuff we never got to at Never Too Late, but the thought of six sets of parents calling the Boys and Girls Club the next day stood between me and a Zen diatribe, so we just stuck to dribbling and passing.

I went through the basics of ball handling, especially about not looking down at the ball. We dribbled backwards, we dribbled forwards, we dribbled with our left hand and our right, we kept our eyes up. Then we worked on passing, chest and bounce. I put them in pairs and had them pass the ball back and forth, watching Allison, the surly one, throw unnecessarily hard to her giggling partner. We worked on lay-ups and shot around a little, and then I decided to talk to them about how to play defense. I asked them if they knew where to look, and they shouted, "The ball!" "Their eyes!" "Their feet!" I told them what I'd told Rolando back at Wicker Park: look at the belly, because they can't fake you out with their belly.

Except for shooting, we'd pretty much covered the game of basketball. I looked at my watch and became traumatized to see that only twenty-five minutes had gone by, and we were out of drills. I sent them out for a drink and frantically thought up a plan for the second half of practice.

When they got back, we played some one-on-one. Ten minutes went by. I sent them out for another drink, which took up another thirty seconds, and then we sat down to talk about our team name.

We were listed as team number 65 at the Boys and Girls Club, and I joked that the name seemed to lack a certain pizzazz. My "humor" provoked stone-faced looks from every girl except Beth, the tomboy, who started laughing and saying, "Number sixty-five! Yeah! Team Sixty-Five, the Sixty-Fives!"

It was the first of many times I was to witness a phenomenon that was sure to bring practice to a halt: Beth talking.

"Go, Sixty-Fives, go! Last year, there was this team, they were called the Ravens, and they were all, like, fashionable, and they had these uniforms with all this stuff all over them and they thought they were so, like, hot, with their warm-up drills and everything, but they cheated, because the refs, like, called everything for them and they always won."

"Really?!" I said, and lined them up by height for some three-on-three. As they played, I was proud to see they were all smiles, having fun, working hard. I asked them once if they needed a break, and they all said no, they wanted to keep playing.

When our time was up, I brought them all back in to huddle and told them they'd done well, good job. Then I asked them what our goal was for the season.

"Play good defense!"

"Win games!"

"Have fun!"

It was Beth who had listened.

I asked them if we'd met our goal for the day, and they all nodded and said yes, except Tonya, who shrugged and held up a thumb and finger by way of saying maybe a little bit.

Standing in the warm glow of the team's good humor, I wanted to give Tonya's ponytail a good, hard yank.

We broke for the night, and as I made my way across the floor, the parents swarmed, introducing themselves and asking questions. As I spoke to one, the others listened a little too hard, looking at me like I was a magician and they were waiting for a trick, and they'd seen lots of tricks before.

It was raining. Beth's dad said, "Okay, Beth, focus! Let's run to the car!" and the two of them took off.

Tonya's stepmom approached me, lugging the carrier. The baby was awake, squirming happily under a blanket. I asked her how old the child was, and the stepmom's countenance softened a shade as she told me twelve weeks. I asked if he'd had colic. "Oh no," she said, "I don't want him to get none of that stuff; that's why I've got him bundled up like this."

Even I knew colic wasn't something you caught like a cold. I looked at the peaceful little boy and wondered briefly about the benefit of not overthinking things, but driving home, a nagging discomfort lingered. Next time, more drills.

Coach Danner, that prince, used to toughen us up at the beginning of a season by putting us in two lines, rolling a ball down the center of the floor, and having us run and dive for it. More often than not, the two girls would reach the ball at the same time and fight for it like gamecocks. We pulled each other's hair, clothes even came off a few times, and for days we'd be proud of our bruises, as if, like Allison's firebomb passes, they made us good players.

Early season included a weigh-in. One year, Coach put poor fat Nicole Burns on the scale and made her cry by calling out her weight in front of the boys' coaches and laughing. The rest of us had bruises that didn't make us better at basketball, but at least they went away.

Six players showed up for the next practice, along with Felicia's mother, Patty, who was dressed out in sweats. She said she'd like to help us, if that was okay, and I said sure it was.

This time I was armed with enough *Baffled* drills to get through two practices. We started with the slide drill, an old defensive standard where one girl faces the rest of the group and leads them in sideways footwork. Then the leader yells "Switch!" and everyone slides the other way. I showed them how to do the drill, put one of the girls in front as leader, and then moved to the back. As we began, I watched Patty among the group, looking like some college starter. I asked her to get up there, please Patty, and show 'em how it's done, and she did; she jumped up and showed them a little perfection, smiling, conscious as a cheerleader of the message in her movements, her knees bent, feet moving, fingers telling her imaginary man, *Come on, come on, just try and drive by me.*

I thought of Steve, the coach at Never Too Late, as I found myself saying, "Now that's what defense *looks* like!"

Then, standing behind all the girls and watching them watch Patty, I saw something. Every cheesy sports movie has the kid with the bad attitude, the one with talent sure to be wasted unless some dedicated coach knocks that chip off and gains his trust and turns him into a team player. It was a cliché, but nonetheless, my bad attitude player was emerging, called on to play her role as surely as the alpha male or the scapegoat in a wolf pack.

Of course it was Tonya lazily going back and forth, legs straight, looking around like she was bored, while the rest of us gladly hopped a ride on Patty's happy train.

I shouted, "Let's see you move, Tonya!" and she started trying, but only for a few minutes before lazing it up again. In the stands, her parents glowered at nothing in particular, the stepmom in her belted leather jacket, the dad in his skullcap. They looked like some terminally pissed-off members of the mod squad with an infant carrier.

When we finished the drill, I had the girls gather around, and I felt hyper-aware of little pockets of feeling all over the gym. Tonya's bored-looking, wandering eyes felt one way. Patty's affirming nods felt another way. In between them was me, the one in charge of creating a reality.

Patty had a way of appearing when we needed her and leaving the floor to me when it was time. She was prone to giving her daughter quick, spontaneous hugs on the court, but once, when Felicia hurt herself and started to cry, Patty wouldn't hug her or even look at her, telling her to shake it off, deal with it.

I had enough drills to make it through practice, but I was still a little relieved when the custodian who monitored the gym got my attention and pointed at his watch. As I headed for the exit, Beth sprinted over to me, shoved a homemade Christmas card into my hand without saying a word, and took off running after her mother. Then I drove home.

• • •

The next practice found our town in the middle of a flu epidemic. Only two players made it: Brittany, whom I was meeting for the first time, and Tonya.

Brittany was skinny as a lizard, and very pretty. She was early, and she immediately asked me if there was a girl from her school named Tonya Greer on our team. When I said yes, she yelled, "I hate that kid! She is such a brat! She won't listen to you, you know, she never listens to anybody. She has to go out in the hall all the time."

"She didn't seem so bad to me," I lied.

I talked to Brittany's mother as she worked to keep the reins on Brittany's second-grade brother, Gordon, and their two-year-old baby sister. The mom apologized for missing the first two practices and cataloged all the running around she'd had to do that day for the kids' events. It was a lot, the mother said, with a two-year-old and living thirty minutes away.

"My husband tells me I'm crazy to let them do all this stuff," she said. "But I don't want it to be like it was for me growing up, with the way my dad was. He took me out of basketball because I complained once, and he took me out of gymnastics because my sister was better than I was."

A stray ball bounced over and hit the two-year-old in the back of the head, nearly knocking her down. The child wailed as I rejoined Brittany out on the court. Tonya arrived, and Brittany gave her a caustic look to let her know how bad it was to see her.

Since we only had two, the coach of the team that had been practicing before us asked us to play with his third-grade girls. "It'll be chaos, no matter what," the coach laughed. Tonya and Brittany were put on teams, along with Brittany's brother Gordon, to even out the sides.

Tonya scored lots of points against the younger, much shorter girls, and with every bucket, she stuck two V for Victory fingers in the air in an unjustified show of cockiness. I watched Brittany closely, since I'd never seen her play before, trying to determine what areas she would need work in, but every aspect of her game appeared equally abysmal as she moved up and down the court, regal and confident and entirely unskilled.

Finally a woman with a distinctly irritated-wife demeanor came over and had a word with the other coach. He shouted, "This is the last time down, girls!"

I wasn't sure what I was going to do with Brittany and Tonya, two girls of drastically different height and experience who couldn't stand the sight of each other, so I grabbed up Gordon and put him on my team for some two-on-two. Brittany made it clear she would have liked to see her brother join Tonya in disappearing.

As we played, a dramatic change in demeanor came over Gordon. After his competent performance in the five-on-five game, he was now unable to remain upright. He toppled on every play, rolling around on the floor massaging his ankles, clutching his wrists, or cupping his nose in a show of athletic agony. I knew he wasn't hurt, but I didn't know what to do with him short of calling for a stretcher, so I suggested maybe he'd like to sit out for a while.

Brittany screamed across the gym, "*Mom!* Gordon's being a big *baby!*"

Their mom walked across the court to check on her son, the still-sniffling toddler hanging on her neck.

"Maybe he's too tired, and that's why he keeps getting hurt," she said, leading him back to the bleachers and quickly rolling her eyes over Brittany's way as if to agree, yes, he's being a big baby, but let's try and be nice. Gordon limped over to the bleachers, no doubt hearing the roar of an imaginary crowd recognizing his bravery.

Brittany, herself not quite over the flu, kept sprinting without warning to the bathroom, leaving me on the court with Tonya, who walked over and talked to her dad during these many breaks. I had no control over anything that was happening.

After Brittany returned from a particularly long absence, Gordon ran back on the court, ready to play through his injuries. It was him and me against the girls, who did everything they could to avoid passing the ball to each other, a unique challenge to infuse into a game of two-on-two. To encourage a pass, I left Tonya wide open in the lane, but Brittany dribbled and dribbled and dribbled. Since she couldn't get by Gordon and wouldn't pass, her only choice was to move backwards, and the two of them began to move away from us. I started hollering at Brittany to pass the ball and come on back, but Gordon was sticking his sister big-time, and she dribbled past the half-court and made it to the out-of-bounds line on the other side. Then she took off for the other half of the gym.

Tonya looked at me and said, "What the . . . ?"

I sighed and said, "I know, I know, I'll get them back down here." To be frank, I was getting pretty tired of this particular practice, but I wasn't going to quit early, especially after hearing all the effort Brittany's mom went to just to get her there.

I'd learned in my earlier practices to keep an eye on the custodian, who sat in a folding chair off by himself and watched the court. Every few minutes he'd yawn and say, "Lord, I'm tired!" but he always perked up when it was time to go home.

Sometimes, when our practice was going well, the custodian sat in his chair a little more alert, cocking his head or smiling a little, and when I saw him like that, I knew our team's energy was positive, that something was *happening*. It was great when I saw that. It wasn't the sublime loss of self that I'd always chased as a player, but it was still great.

Now the custodian slept like a dead canary in a coal mine. The building was almost empty, and the echoing sounds of Brittany's too-distant dribbling felt surreal as a fever dream. I felt very noticed, like a rabbit in the middle of a prairie, and then, suddenly, the custodian stood, caught my attention, pointed at his watch, and grinned like he knew he was saving me.

Leaving the gym, I mentioned to Brittany's mom something about we'd have more players next time and it would be more organized. "That's okay, this is what she needs, one-on-one attention," she said. She might have been kind, or she might have been embarrassed by her kids' behavior, with her unlucky two-year-old, the son with his agony of defeat, and her smart-mouthed, bathroom-dwelling daughter. I wondered how strong her resolve would remain not to have it be like it was for her in the face of such an onslaught.

Tonya's father approached and alternately cooed into the infant carrier and told me about his own stellar high school and college basketball career, and that of Tonya's mother.

"We keep trying to beat it through Tonya's head how talented she is, but she doesn't realize it. She didn't even want to play for a while, so we said, 'Okay, do what you want,' and now she's out here again."

So far I hadn't seen that Tonya was talented at anything other than being big, but her dad seemed to believe she was born good at basketball, and if she didn't live up to her genes, it could only be a character flaw.

Tonya hung close, listening but acting like she wasn't. I remembered that shrug of hers from the first practice, when I'd asked them if they'd had fun. Possibly, it was the best she could do.

It was the day before our first game, and my mind was filled with disconcerting images from our three practices. Amanda running with the basketball like a quarterback. Brittany's audible slapping fouls. Tonya strolling down the court as the rest of the team got back on defense.

During practice I'd say, "Remember to dribble!" and "Don't dribble so much! Pass the ball!" I'd say, "Don't touch the other person!" and then later, when someone put their body on someone else on defense, I'd try to explain why that wasn't a foul. "Let's hustle!" I'd holler at Tonya, and then to Beth, "Slow down, be a little more patient."

Basketball is a hard game to explain.

I tried to believe that the girls didn't always do what I said because maybe ten-year-olds don't have good self-control, or maybe they just forgot once they got out on the court and things started moving fast. So I'd remind them fifty times, hoping it would sink in on the fifty-first time.

It was a league rule that everyone had to get equal minutes during games, so I wouldn't be able to bench someone for anything, including blatant insubordination. The buzzer would sound every four minutes for substitutions, and players would stay in the game until it was their turn to come out.

Sitting in my house thinking about our practices, I became less and less charitably inclined toward my team. All I could do was beg, and they knew it, the little hussies.

I was relieved on Saturday morning to see six of our seven players: enough to man the floor, with one sub. Standing on the sidelines waiting for the game before ours to end were Beth, Amanda, Felicia, Emily, Brittany, and Allison. When they saw me, they came running, excited and jumping around like fleas.

No Tonya. That was odd, since I'd called all the parents the day before, and Tonya's dad hadn't said anything about not coming.

The players were so proud of their green T-shirts with a number on the back that I couldn't help but feel kindly toward them again.

We warmed up by milling about and bricking free throws, while the dozen players on the other end ran a fancy warm-up drill. I called the team in to huddle, and I said to them, now, you're not nervous, are you? They all said no, except Felicia, who nodded her head and said uuuuu-huuuuh, she was scared. She twitched a little, and her eyes were wide and round. I told Felicia I was a little nervous, too. And I was, looking up into the crowded bleachers.

Somebody asked where Tonya was, and Beth informed us that Tonya's dad was going to get her on another team, a team that would have thirteen players if she joined. This possibility pissed me off at the dad and the Boys and Girls Club both, so I tried not to think about it right then.

I mentioned that Emily would do the jump ball.

"What's a jump ball?!" Brittany shrieked.

Although she had claimed not to be nervous, she sounded panicked.

"It's how they start the game," I said. "Don't worry about it, it's not hard, and you'll see how it works."

"I want to practice a jump ball now!" Brittany hollered.

"No, not now, when the game starts," I said, yelling over the other team's well-rehearsed pregame chant, and understanding that they were going to kill us.

Before I'd spoken for ten more seconds, I'd mentioned another technical term unfamiliar to Brittany.

"What's a buzzer?!"

"You know what a buzzer is, you silly thing."

I poked her in the side and said, "What's a shirt? What are shoes? Where's my head?"

The team was giggling as they headed out onto the floor, which wasn't the ideal attitude, but at least it was better than being stiff with fear.

The ref helped everyone set up for the jump ball, and Emily got the tip to Brittany, who took off dribbling. On the way down, Brittany's defender got too close and perhaps grazed her hand, because Brittany picked up the ball, extended the girl a hateful glare, and then took off dribbling again. When the refs didn't call the blatant traveling violation, I realized I'd placed way too much focus, or roughly a third of our practice time, on the finer points of ball handling.

Our bigger problem was that we had no offense. Allison made our first bucket, a miracle thrown up from the corner of the lane. It was unfortunate her shot went in, because it meant she felt justified shooting every time she got the ball.

If the officiating wasn't exactly rigorous, it was consistent, but the girls complained about fouls at our substitution breaks, saying that the other team was beating them up and the refs weren't calling it. I said the reffing was fine, and there was nothing I could do about it anyway, and they needed to focus on their game. Brittany asked me if I couldn't yell at them.

"You don't want me to get a technical, do you?"

"Oh noooo," she said reverently, surely having no idea what I was talking about.

Having a good attitude and being anxious to please may have been desirable attributes in practice, but they were entirely useless when it came time to play. Emily, Felicia, and Amanda—my angels of sanity—stood back and watched rebounds fall in front of them as if they had no hands. Unless the ball arrived in the form of a delicate pass intended only for their receipt, they didn't bother with it, apparently under the impression that it would be impolite to steal the ball or be grabby about it.

Beth and Allison and Brittany were everywhere. They may not have always known *what* they were doing, but whatever it was, they were on it, asking for the pass, taking shots, mixing it up, and working hard.

Prissy Brittany rolled on the floor after loose balls in between adjusting her headband so much that I half-expected her to pull a hand mirror out of her sock and check her look as she ran down court.

Beth was everything you could want: aggressive, smart, confident. She kept us in the game, and as we came back from halftime, we were only three points behind.

But then, from out of nowhere came number five, with three lay-ups straight in a row. I told Beth, momentarily benched, to guard the girl when she went back in. When it was time, Beth ran into the game, anxious as a thoroughbred to get out there. She stuck number five admirably—too admirably and too close actually, and the girl drove past her, carrying the ball five steps before tossing in her lay-ups.

In practice, I'd talked to the team about playing defense, about how, if you stand too close, your girl can drive past you, and if you stand too far back, she can take the outside shot. My first game taught me that there was no outside shot in fourth-grade basketball; it was the nondribbling drive that would bite you in the ass.

We lost, twenty to ten.

When the final buzzer sounded, Gordon appeared at my side, ready to extend his condolences after our crushing defeat.

"It's okay," he said, taking on a mature, experienced air that seemed as studied as his phantom injuries. "Your team worked hard, and they played a good game. It doesn't matter that you got stomped. All that matters is you tried your best."

I told Gordon he was right about that and thanked him for his well-chosen words.

Beth's dad avoided the parent surge, but I ran into him on the way out. He was leaning on a door facing, as if he'd been waiting on me. "Well," he said, "not too bad, considering everybody's been sick."

I said yeah, the girls had hung in there, and I mentioned how I'd put Beth on number five, letting him know that I knew Beth was my best player. The dad had never remarked on Beth's GLA status, but you'd have to be blind not to see she had something. Short, pudgy, and self-effacing, Beth's dad didn't give the impression of someone with a stellar athletic past, and he made a small joke about Beth's not getting her talent from him. I was beginning to suspect that his watchful, laissez-faire bemusement was part of what allowed Beth to find her own talent, then flourish.

"We'll get better," I said, hoping Beth and her family would accept her solid position as star of a ragtag team.

"Oh, it's just a game," he said, laughing. I could feel that he was on my side, like Gordon, like the custodian, like Patty. They couldn't have known how much they mattered to me, just being who they were.

I drove home with Bill the boyfriend. He said what I really needed was a better warm-up drill. It was an accurate if not comprehensive analysis.

The next week, I spent a good bit of time with this new book Bill bought for me called *Coaching Basketball.* I was especially interested in learning how to get across the concept of the rebound. There was a whole chapter on it, and reading about the perfect form—elbows out, feet wide, head up, aggressive yet poised enough to evaluate what was happening on the floor—I wanted to go out and tear down a few myself.

There were so many arrows and circles in the offense chapter that I decided a simple moratorium on outside shooting would be sufficient for the time being. Better shot selection, joined with half a chance at a rebound—that was the plan.

When I got to practice, Patty and most of my players were sitting on the bottom row of bleachers. The other parents sat in the rows just behind them, turning their heads in unison to look at me as I walked in. They could've had a caption under them: "Now what?"

I did my best impression of confidence and had Patty and the players gather around. I told them what our focus would be for practice: offense, rebounding, and aggressiveness. These were the things we needed to work on the most, the things we hadn't focused on enough before our first game. I wanted them to think there was a simple explanation for losing so badly, and what's more, I knew what it was and how to fix it.

Tonya wasn't there. I put Beth and Emily in the lane and called everyone else a guard. Then I preached a sermon on shot selection.

"Our goal on offense," I harped, "is to get the ball inside for the high percentage shot. That's our goal on *offense*," I restated, "to get the ball inside. We have to take shots that have the *greatest likelihood* of going in, so no shooting from any further out than here."

I dragged my foot along the edge of the lane for emphasis.

"Everybody got it?"

"I made my shot! My shot went in!" Allison shouted, referring to the freakish two points she'd scored, which, no doubt, she'd been replaying in her head at every opportunity since the game.

I told her I knew it did, but we wanted to increase our chances of scoring *more often* by taking shots closer in. Allison looked crestfallen, like she was never going to have another star moment on the court.

"It's okay," I said. "We'll still get fast breaks, and the guards will get inside sometimes, too. Just work with me on this for now, okay?"

She nodded.

We ran our simple offense for a while, and I stopped them every few minutes to ask, "What's our goal on offense?"

"Score points!" someone shouted.

"Make good passes!" someone else yelled.

"Get the ball inside!" Beth said.

Tonya showed up, looking hesitant on the sidelines, like some-one who didn't know if she belonged or not. Her dad was in the bleachers, sans baby, paying full attention to what was happening on the court. This was serious business.

I told her to hang tight, and I'd get her on the court in a few minutes.

Every few plays I'd stop the girls and ask them what our goal was on offense. "Get the ball inside!" they all began to say. I was re-ally drumming it into their heads.

Patty played, helping anyone who seemed confused, pushing them lightly in the right direction and saying, "Go this way," or "Move away from your pass."

We stayed with our offense for a half-hour, and it was working. The guards were looking inside instead of trying to shoot all the time, the ball was actually getting in to Beth and Emily, and they were hitting a few. The vibe was good, the players were energized, the parents were watching, the custodian was awake, even Tonya was working hard. For the moment, I was the one with the an-swers, the woman with the plan, and I decided to move on to re-bounding while I was ahead.

We'd practiced boxing out in our earlier practices, but our first game had made it clear these lessons didn't stick. I'd jumped the gun, I thought, talking about getting in position before I'd shown them something about rebounding form.

I talked about the elbows swinging and the wide feet and the looking around. When we started a drill, most of the girls swung their arms all right, after standing flat-footed and waiting for the ball to come down like a pop fly. The problem was even more basic than form. The problem was they didn't know to time it so they got the ball at the highest point of their jump. So I stopped the drill and scaled things back even more. I started throwing the ball in the air to the girls one at a time, away from the hoop and with-out a defender, so they could focus on timing and nothing else.

That seemed to work: they started *looking* like rebounders. Patty and I broke into groups and helped them practice jumping.

Gradually we worked our way back to the hoop, and then we put in a defensive player. It was time to talk about being aggressive. I stopped practice again for a short sermon on how girls are expected to be well mannered and polite, but a great thing about basketball is that it's one time that you don't have to be nice. "You don't need to worry about your table manners out here," I said, hamming it up, swaggering a little, making Patty laugh. "Don't worry about bein' *nice* out here on the court. That's not what it's about today."

The players seemed to be almost prancing, like horses before a storm, and I felt like Tina Turner back in the Ike days, doing her talky, preachy intro to "Proud Mary" where she says, as the band starts to feel it, "A lot of people have sung this song, and we're gonna sing it, too, but we're not gonna sing it *nice*." It was a subversive gospel, trying to convince ten-year-old girls that nice wasn't all they were made of.

"We're not gonna get hurt out here, but we're not gonna worry about hurting someone's *feelings* by taking the ball away from her either. Isn't that right, Patty?"

"That's right!" Patty said, and it seemed like she was glad for her daughter to be hearing the word.

Then Patty took the ball and shot to miss, and two players at a time worked for the rebound. Before I knew it, pairs of girls were rolling around on the floor tussling for the ball, and I had to keep breaking up the struggles, saying, "Okay, good hustle, good job, that's a jump, okay, next two." I didn't want them actually fighting, just working hard for possession, and I was a little surprised, to tell the truth, at how quickly they'd taken to the aggression message. Maybe all they'd needed to break out—to want something, to go for it with their feet and hands and arms and everything they had —maybe all they'd needed, if you can believe it, was *permission*.

From that moment on, I was coaching.

• • •

We had a second, optional practice scheduled for the next Friday, the night before our second game. I planned to repeat most of the earlier practice, assuming the girls would have forgotten everything by game time.

Tonya's dad made his first appearance on the floor, leaving the baby in the bleachers asleep in the carrier, to help us work on our offense. He took it upon himself to be my slack, and in the face of any giggling or whispering, he would yell, "Come on, girls, listen to your coach!"

He was tall and ominous, and the girls snapped to attention when he hollered, but after the fear wore off, they became even gigglier.

I tended to overlook most of the girls' horseplay. Not Tonya's dad—that dude ran a tight ship.

"Can I say something?" he asked me after a few plays. I thought he would have some advice about positioning or shot selection.

"Sure," I said.

"Listen up!" he yelled, silencing the girls and causing the baby to flinch in his sleep. "It's time for you girls to get serious and quit goofing off! Now is the time to get good at this game if you want to play in college someday! Now is the time to learn this stuff, before it's too late! Now! Are you going to get out there tomorrow and act silly and ridiculous, or are you going to act like players?"

He looked around at them as if his question weren't rhetorical.

"Well, which is it?"

A few of the girls shook their heads back and forth or mumbled, "Players."

"Now don't just throw the ball up any old way without thinking about what you're doing! Your coach told you where you could shoot, and if you're not where she said, then *don't shoot!*"

He gave me a "that's how you do it" look as the girls scrambled back to their positions, and when we began playing again, they got rid of the ball like they were afraid of it, refusing to shoot from anywhere. I let them run the play a few more times before telling them to go take a break. When they came back, I put them in single file near the free throw line and had them come in for lay-ups as I passed the ball to them.

Tonya came in for her turn and threw the ball up with an awkward underhanded motion, missing the entire basket. Watching her act silly and ridiculous about the miss, I got the impression she was mishandling the lay-up intentionally, maybe for attention, or maybe because, as long as she hauled out one of her infinite impressions of "I don't care," no one would notice she didn't know how to do something.

Her dad scoffed. "Tonya, come on, you know how to shoot a lay-up." He really didn't seem to like her very much.

We spent the rest of practice working on a new drill to use for a simple game warm-up, and afterwards, I thanked Tonya's dad without inviting him back, then hurriedly asked about the baby. "Oh, he's a good boy," the dad said. "Nothing like how Tonya was when she was a baby. She was a whiner. Still is."

Tonya stood on the periphery, hearing but not hearing.

Later, when I told Bill the boyfriend about the dad's tirades, he said, "Good. That's what a coach does, he yells. He's a coach, not a friend."

Possibly he had a point, but even on the off chance he was right, you shouldn't *enjoy* yelling as much as Tonya's dad seemed to. You shouldn't get intoxicated by the sound of your own powerful words.

Tonya's dad didn't ask to help again that season, and I was glad.

We did our new warm-up before the next game. It was nothing fancy, just two lines, one passing, one going in for lay-ups, but it made us look reasonably competent.

The buzzer sounded, and as we started playing, something happened to me. When one of the girls threw up a prayer, all I had to say was "Shot selection!" and that was enough. I demanded they work for rebounds, and I got a little pissed when they didn't stay on their girl. I could praise them, too, and know that I wasn't just cheering from the sidelines. Self-consciousness was gone. It didn't matter anymore who was watching, and I was able to treat the girls like they were accountable and not fragile. I'm sure I looked pretty unattractive out there hollering, making faces I probably wouldn't want to see, and enjoying the freedom of not knowing what I might do next.

We took the lead, and we stayed ahead, and the game felt like riding a horse that could either buck me off or suddenly vanish out from underneath me. It had to be managed, hung on to moment by moment.

Tonya's dad sat on the bottom bleacher, absently rocking the baby's carrier with one hand and never letting up on Tonya. At one of our substitution breaks, Tonya ran over and complained, "I can't concentrate . . . my dad is yelling too much!"

It was one of her more direct cries for help. I said, "That's okay. Just try to put it out of your mind," and I think she did try.

When I met the dad's eyes once, he gave me a thumbs-up and grin showing all his teeth. He was giddy as hell, now that we were winning.

And we did it. We stayed ahead, and when we won, the girls yelled and the parents cheered and it was all a blur except for one very small moment of intense clarity when Beth's dad found a second to look me in the eye and say, "*You* are a good coach." He said it quietly, without a trace of his usual irony, and his blue eyes were newly noticeable as he seemed to search mine for confirmation of something he now suspected.

We all have our moments.

In the days following our *second* victory, I became prone to telling innocent bystanders about the team, which was now calling itself the Ball Hawgs.

"How's it going?" a coworker would ask, meaning *in general,* and I'd say well, did you know the fourth-grade girls' basketball team I'm coaching is two and one?

"Wow, really? That's great," the waitress would say, thinking that was the end of that as I stared off into space, gearing up to utter a wealth of sentences beginning, "You know, the key is . . ." or

"The thing to remember about this age group . . ." or "My own theory. . . "

I'd stand up tall, stopping just short of hiking up my pants, anxious to explain a success I found inexplicable.

As we warmed up for our fourth game, I overheard Beth reporting that Tonya's stepmother was so mad at Tonya for fighting at school that she might not be back for like the whole year.

Amanda was missing, too, leaving us with only five Ball Hawgs.

So far, each of our opponents had substantially outnumbered us, but I thought our small roster reduced mayhem and wasn't a disadvantage as long as we had at least one sub. We wouldn't for this game.

There was a league rule that any team with ten or more players could request an extra four-minute period to give everyone more playing time. The other team's coach took this option, so we had nine four-minute periods ahead of us. To make matters worse, standing out among the dozen girls warming up on the other end was a player so big and solid and menacing, she seemed like a redwood tree compared to our team of decorative Bradford pears.

I called the girls around to huddle and reminded them about shot selection and hustling for the ball. As I saw them cutting glances toward the other team, I said they'd been outnumbered the week before, and the five we had were our starters for that game, and look how we did, which didn't really mean anything, but it sounded good.

I mentioned that Beth would jump.

"I want to do the jump ball!"

"*Sweetie,*" I said to Brittany, "the tallest girls do the jump because they're the ones who have the best chance at getting it."

"Oh," Brittany said.

The big girl used her two-inch vertical leap to bat the ball easily to a teammate, but after a few plays, it was apparent that the girl's size was the only real advantage she had. The poor thing was slow as a redwood, too.

Beth kicked ass to an even greater extent than usual, scoring, rebounding, getting steals, and making good passes. Our star player was talented, pure and simple, but she also listened and worked hard, she wasn't small or timid, and she was well liked by the other players. There was nothing stopping her.

I thought of our strategy as a solar system offense, with Beth as the sun. She generally threw the ball in and helped the guards get the ball down court by moving constantly to stay open, so when a teammate picked up her dribble and got stuck, Beth was there to bail her out. Then, once we made it down and things were relatively stabilized, Beth headed for the post area, where she usually got the ball for the shot and, if she missed, was likely to get the rebound.

It wasn't the sort of thing you'd find in a book, but it worked.

Allison's game wasn't as comprehensive as Beth's, but she was the second most powerful member of our team. She played strong defense, and she was an outstanding passer, but from the woeful looks she gave me when I bragged on her, I gathered that she took her gift for granted, and the feeling of a beautiful assist couldn't compare to sinking a shot.

With no subs, we maintained a modest lead throughout the game, and with three periods left, we were ahead by six. We had the advantage, but when the girls came over to huddle, they looked exhausted and a little desperate, like it wouldn't take much for the momentum to change, and if it did, fatigue might get the better of them.

I told them to pay attention, because I had a plan. I began to speak very slowly and punch my words like a newsreader.

"Now listen, everybody. Because we're ahead and we're tired, I want us to do something. For the next four minutes, on *offense*, I want you all to pass and pass and pass, and don't take any shots unless you're just wide open. Just pass and pass and pass, for as long as you can. What I'm saying is, we want to run time off the clock, and that's why I'm telling you not to shoot, okay? Just pass and pass and pass, and really limit your shooting. That's my point here. This isn't how we're going to play *from now on,* but it's how we need to play *right now*, because we want to maintain our lead, and we need to conserve our energy and not run up and down the court so much. Okay? Everybody got it? What'd I just say?"

I went around the circle, making the five of them say it back to me. Pass the ball, slow down the game. Pass the ball, slow down the game. Pass the ball, slow down the game.

The buzzer sounded. Beth took the ball out on our end and passed it in to Allison, who promptly shot an air ball from her favorite position three feet outside the lane. The other team got the ball, ran down court, and scored. Ten seconds had elapsed.

"Allison!"

She ignored me.

"*Allison!*"

She looked over with her head down and her eyes up. I didn't say much beyond giving her a confused, palms-up shoulder shrug, like I was a little hurt.

The refs allowed coaches to step out on the court "for instruction" as long as we didn't interfere with the game, and I always took advantage of this rule in lieu of a team prescription for Ritalin. For the remainder of that period, I maintained a position four feet inside the out-of-bounds line, and I ran up and down the court with my team, shouting, as we came down on offense, "Remember what we're doing!" "Remember what we said about the clock!" "Pass it pass it pass it!" "Don't forget!"

And they did it: they passed the ball, worked our stall plan, took a few good shots here and there. At the end of the period, we were eight points ahead, and the girls didn't seem so frantic and tired.

"Did that seem to work?" I asked, rubbing it in a little.

Beth nodded and said yeah, it did, and I told them well, all right, then, let's do it again.

My favorite ref was calling the game. He was awake-looking and well over seventeen years old, which singled him out among the shaggy, unenthusiastic high school boys who typically called our games. He made sure the girls had found their matchups before he started the play, and he coaxed players out of running with the ball, saying, "Come on now, you gotta dribble a *little* bit." When a girl held on to the ball too long, he encouraged the other girls to grab it away, promoting a healthy aggressiveness and keeping the game going.

Once, when the big redwood girl got the ball and hung on, Brittany got her in a mean-faced tugging match. Brittany looked like a chipmunk wrestling a bear, but she hung on, and when the whistle blew, she let go, a little confused, like she was thinking, *Was that me? Did I do that?*

She looked at the big girl, and then she looked at me. I laughed a little and clapped just for Brittany and praised her. I could almost hear her thoughts: *Damn, I'm aggressive.* She seemed calm, an uncharacteristic countenance for Brittany, and happy.

I glanced into the stands. Beth's dad laughed and gave Brittany's mom a light punch on the arm. The mom, who had told me recently that Brittany's tae kwon do coach had suggested she try St. John's Wort, shook her head and smiled with qualified pride. Gordon was right there, wearing Ball Hawg green and swirling a noise-maker.

We managed to keep things slowed down, and by the end of the period, our win was pretty much in the bank. I got off their backs a little for the final four minutes, and we won, twenty-three to sixteen.

When the game was over, the girls stood around me while I told them they were amazing, incredible, unbelievable, all the words you use to describe great women. Then I stepped outside the gym, and I had to blink a little, in the sudden daylight and solitude, like leaving a theater after a good movie.

Every close game had a turning point that allowed us a few moments to get our brains right or start losing. The first sign was a panic that came over the girls' faces when the other team had a run and we felt a lack of control, the coming of our own relinquishment. After a few games, the emerging panic was familiar to me. I recognized it, and I knew, when I saw it on my players' faces and felt it in myself, that it was not time to nag the girls about turnovers, but to help them manage their chaos and vulnerability. When the win hung in the air, preexistent and waiting for someone to snatch it, it wasn't about what they were doing as much as what they were thinking.

One of those moments came in the seventh period of the fifth game, with the score tied. The other team had started doubling up on our guards at the half-court line, leaving the rest of our players open but impossible to access, and after a few turnovers, I saw that panic.

It was a league rule that there were no timeouts until the final period, so I couldn't do much to break the momentum or talk to my team at any length. All I could do was walk out on the court a few extra feet to make sure the girls could hear me shout the words I hoped might make a difference. "It's okay," "We're doing fine," "Let's calm down and focus," "It's okay . . . we're okay."

Allison had hurt herself early in the game, so I'd taken her out temporarily when I wasn't planning to. This had altered my lineup, resulting, now, in a situation I tried to avoid: Beth and Allison sitting out at the same time. I walked over to the two of them and said get ready, because I knew they were going to make a difference when they got in there. I could see them scramble a little at my words as they prepared for action, feeling proud to have confidence placed in them. I'd meant what I said, but it felt a little manipulative to try to control their mindset like that, like something a preacher or a politician might do.

We were behind by six when the last four-minute period started and Beth and Allison went in. For a while, things remained as pell-mell as ever, even with my two best players in the game. You could tell by their faces, even Beth's, that my team was ready to lose.

I called my only timeout. The girls came over and huddled around, crazed, wild-eyed, shouting about this or that.

"Everybody put your hands in here," I said, sticking my own hand in the middle of our circle. A few of them quieted, while others continued to shout.

"*Shhhhh*, nobody say anything. I want you to all be quiet and focus for a minute."

Allison kept on until I touched her mouth lightly and said *shhh-shhh-shhh*, like I was soothing a baby. She gave up and hushed.

I said it again. "Nobody say anything. Let's all be quiet for just a second, please. Just focus and be silent for a few seconds."

Possibly they were going to think I was a big dumb-ass, but I didn't care. I glanced at Beth, who had gone so far as to close her eyes. As usual, she was listening, taking what I said and making it her own, wanting, more than anything else, to play better and win, and willing to let me help if I could.

I think that's what the Zen folks call a beginner's mind. It's an amazing thing, especially in someone who's already the best.

I waited a few seconds and said, "It's okay. It's just a game. If we're gonna try and win, we have to stay calm. It's okay."

I smiled at them, hoping that if I didn't seem stressed, they would settle down. I wanted them to remember that what we were trying to hang on to was just a damned fickle win, not love itself, not something vital. I wanted them to believe it, because it was the truth, because it would make them feel better, and because it was our best chance.

Beth opened her eyes and smiled, back to herself. The gym was roaring, but the Ball Hawgs were a circle of quiet. For a blessed moment, we were home, family, relief, and gratitude. We couldn't hear the crowd.

And then, when we got back in, things *were* different. The Ball Hawgs had regained some mastery over themselves, and Beth went crazy getting steals and rebounds and speeding the ball down court for points. There was no doubting that this was her world, and with two minutes left, she had a lot of work to do. The other players, as usual, followed suit.

We were behind by one with ten seconds left, and we had the ball on their end. Felicia passed it in to Beth, who hustled it down court. Seconds were ticking, the crowd was going nuts, and I was screaming, "You have to shoot! You have to shoot it, Beth! *Shoooooot iiiiittttttt!!!!!*"

She took an outside shot with two seconds left, she missed, the buzzer sounded, and the game was over.

We lined up and told the other team good game. When the opposing coach extended his hand, he laughed and said, "It was a barn burner, wasn't it, coach?" It wasn't too hard to take his hand and agree that it sure was.

One night at practice, I was having a harder time than usual getting the girls to listen. As I tried to talk to them about defense, they performed various cheerleader moves, shoved one another around, and played piggyback. I kept saying, "Come on, girls, listen up, please," but they acted pretty much like I wasn't there.

Patty was helping me that night. She looked vacantly into the stands and ambled around, waiting for me to get a handle on the situation.

I started thinking uncharitably toward the little ingrates, inappreciative as they were of my time as a *volunteer* coach, and I said, with what I thought was authority, "Girls! Hush up now, I mean it! I need you to listen!"

They giggled.

"You're acting like a bunch of puppies."

The notion of themselves as dogs was quite hilarious, especially when portrayed by Beth, who got on her knees, put two bent wrists in front of her chest, and began to pant and howl.

Then someone shoved Felicia, and she shoved back, laughing. With this, Patty's reverie came to an abrupt end. She gave her daughter a lethal mother-look that silenced not only Felicia but the rest of the team as well. To my astonishment, not only did the team get quiet, *they stood at attention.*

"All right then," I said, trying to shake off a feeling of exhaustion. "Let's work on this defense."

We won the next game, making our record four and two. The week after that, I was standing on the sidelines waiting for our seventh game to start when two skinny arms entwined themselves around my waist. After several seconds of Brittany's clinging like an infant monkey, I began to feel embarrassed. I gently pried her off.

Tonya, apparently out on early parole, had reappeared the previous week. Between her scouting other teams and getting in trouble, her presence at games and practices had been spotty and tense all season, but today she was all smiles, and she said to me, in a voice so sweet it made your teeth hurt, "My mom said to tell you thanks."

I'd agreed to give Tonya a ride after the game. God only knows what self-esteem issues made me say I'd do it, when her absence was always good news, and lately she'd taken to crying every time I took her out. It made no difference when I explained the rotation process and told her that everyone got equal playing time because that was the rule, and not even my rule, but the Boys and Girls Club rule.

It was a straightforward concept to everyone but Tonya, who continued to cause a scene when it was her time to come out. For this game, I'd written the lineup down on a piece of paper and taped it to the wall. "Look, everyone," I said, talking to Tonya, "here's today's lineup. Here it is, written down, not gonna change, cut in stone."

Not only was Tonya unable to come to terms with being taken out of the game; she'd also refuse to return to the court four minutes later when it was her turn to get back in the game.

In practice, Tonya was prone to walking off the court any ol' time she felt like it, looking back at me to make sure I was noticing her insubordination. When we worked on a drill, she often took off with the ball and went to shoot on another hoop, leaving me and everyone else standing there looking at her. She complained about who she had to guard, and she complained about who was on her team, and if she fell, she put on a show that would have put even the theatrical Gordon to shame. Every scrape caused Tonya to scream and wail like she was in labor with a twelve-pound baby.

I'd stopped pondering or caring whether Tonya was spoiled, abused, neglected, crazy, or all of the above. In practice, when she'd whine, "I don't want to guard Beth!" I'd say things like, "Really, Tonya, this isn't about what you want." The idea seemed to shock her, and my tone shocked me. I hadn't expected to be snapping at a ten-year-old that way.

I should've known something was up before the game, with Brittany hugging me and Tonya so sticky sweet. A parent or teacher would have recognized such unnatural events as a reason to sniff the air a little harder, but I just thought, Hey, it's really shaping up to be a nice morning.

A ref I'd never seen before approached and began to clue me in on his reffing philosophy. "All right," he drawled, using his tongue to rearrange the wad of smokeless tobacco in his cheek. "The way I do things is, I'm gonna call some walks, and I'm gonna call some fouls. I'm not gonna call every walk, mind you, because you know and I know I can't do that."

He paused, creating a pregnant-with-meaning vibe.

"But I'm gonna call some," he said. "I'm gonna call my share."

"Sounds good to me," I said. "Thanks for letting me know. I'll keep it in mind."

"And another thing, if you have a question about a call, you can ask me, but when I say I've heard enough, then I've heard enough, and I don't wanna hear no more about it."

What in the world did this guy think I was gonna do, throw chairs?

"I understand," I said. "I really do."

Then I told him I liked to run around a lot and get on the court for instruction during the games, and I asked him to just let me know if I got in the way.

"Oh, I'll let you know, so you go on ahead and you do your runnin' around."

We started playing, and after a couple of periods, the note on the wall told me to take Tonya out. "Good job, Tonya," I said as we huddled before the third period. "It's your turn to come out now. Be sure to rest up and get a drink, because you're back in in four minutes."

In the face of my unmitigated cruelty, Tonya stomped into the bleachers above our huddle to sit by Allison's grandparents, who had been kind enough to hold her jacket. She sobbed into her hands while the grandmother rubbed her shoulders.

The game resumed, and with a minute left in the period, I walked over to tell Tonya to get ready, it was almost time to go back in the game. To this, she replied, "I don't want to go back in! I'm not going to play basketball anymore!"

"I think her feelings are hurt," Allison's grandmother whispered carefully. "We've been telling her, 'There is no 'I' in *team*.'"

I resented the old woman unreasonably.

"Listen, Tonya," I said. "I don't have time for this. It's your turn to go in, I want you to go in, but I can't force you to go in. Make up your mind and tell me right now, do you want to play or not?"

"No," she snapped.

"Well, come on, Allison, I know you're ready."

When Tonya saw I wasn't going to get down on my knees and beg, she hopped down out of the bleachers and ran in front of Allison onto the court.

"Allison, you're in at four minutes," I told her, furious at Tonya for making not only me but also Allison feel foolish.

Two periods later, the score was still close and Beth was coming out. This would be our toughest piece of the game, and I was hoping we wouldn't get too far behind to catch up when Beth got back in.

As we huddled and I talked to the team, I felt some sort of sarcastic energy going on beside me, and I looked over just in time to see Tonya mouthing "Little Miss Perfect" at Brittany. Never one to suffer disrespect, Brittany came across the circle of girls and hit Tonya in the face. Tonya hit her back, and before I knew it, they were slapping furiously at each other.

I stood there stunned for a few seconds, doing nothing, like those two middle-aged Park District employees in Chicago, the ones with the ID tags who had said, "Gentleman, gentlemen." Only when Beth jumped in the middle of Tonya and Brittany, looking at me like *Why aren't you* doing *something?* did I get involved, telling Tonya and Brittany to stop it, stop it now, I mean it. I hated my voice, which had the quality of a cop talking to two drunks, trying to sound authoritative instead of disgusted or afraid.

They stopped slapping, and with the ref waiting on us, I quickly finished the now-ironic point I'd been making, that we needed to be more aggressive. "Remember our second game," I said, "the one after we lost, when we were playing so hard and really going for the ball and getting rebounds? We need to get back to that, okay? Got it? Everybody ready?"

The girls nodded and headed onto the court. They found their matchups, and everything was sane until Tonya and Brittany, standing at center court, became stimulated by the sight and proximity of each other.

Unthinkably, Tonya extended a kick to Brittany's shin. Brittany kicked Tonya. They kicked some more, creating a scene that looked less like a fight than a formal exchange of prissy blows.

In the few seconds it took me, again, to stop watching the train wreck and move, the ref was hollering, "Okay, Green, okay now! Let's settle down now, Green!" He scanned the court, finding me and giving me a look similar to Beth's: *Would you do somethin' about this,* coach?

I trotted out to center court, stood between the two contenders, pointed at each of them and said, "No" and "No." I gave them slight shoves in opposite directions and headed back to the sidelines. The ref blew his whistle, and then, I'll be damned if Tonya didn't start making points, grabbing the ball, getting rebounds, and generally playing, for the first time all season, like there was a heart under all that brattiness.

And Brittany was just as powerful. The fight had made her fast and wily, and she was stealing passes with the cool poise of a sniper.

Tonya and Brittany were rolling around on the floor after loose balls, and the ref called the jumps, blowing his whistle and saying, "Okay, okay, girls, easy now, this ain't a street fight." But I liked what the girls were doing, and I said to them, trying not to let the ref hear my subtle contradictions, "It's okay . . . way to be aggressive."

When the period was over, we were ahead by eight, with four minutes to go.

For once, I hated to take Tonya out, but it was her turn. She left the court all peaceable-like and stood by me on the sidelines, perfectly lucid, as we watched the end of the game.

"Listen," I said to her. "Look at that scoreboard. Your team is going to win this game, and it's largely because of you. Doesn't that make you feel kind of proud?"

She nodded, and I hoped that feeling good about herself would seem more appealing than continuing to be such a sizable pain in my ass.

After the game, the girls hung around for a while, giggling and talking to people they knew on other teams. Brittany and Tonya, with their arms slung around each other, begged Brittany's mom to let them have a sleepover.

Brittany noticed me staring at them with my mouth open. "Tonya and I just had that fight to get attention," she explained happily.

Beth's dad stood nearby. I pointed at the two maniacs and looked at him with a question mark.

"Girls," he said, shaking his head.

The ref approached me again, and I readied myself for an exposition on how to handle on-court fights.

"I have two questions for you," he said, "and the answer needs to be yes to both. Are you single, and do you date referees?"

It was a nice, corny way to ask someone out, and I was a little charmed. I noticed details about his appearance for the first time: that he was tall and muscular with a flat stomach, and his teeth were straight and healthy, though yellow with tobacco stains.

I laughed a little and told him I had to admit I wasn't quite single. I asked his name and said he'd done a good job, suspecting that reffing was important to him, and he talked about it a lot, like I talked about volunteer coaching to anyone who would stand still.

That's the trick right there, girls: giving yourself permission to do something noticeable for a purpose other than getting noticed. Take it from someone who has been around long enough to have lost a step: forget what people are thinking about you, every chance you get, every way you can.

Coaching changed the way I played. During a game or just shooting around, I'd find myself thinking about somebody's attitude and what he could do to improve. Once, I went to the Jones Center, and I was matched up against a girl who was five inches taller and much stronger than I was. She was also about twenty years old and, as I'd seen while we warmed up, a good outside shooter. *And* she had unshaven armpits. She was pretty intimidating, and I prepared to play and get my butt kicked in a two-on-two game with the girl's boyfriend and another guy.

But the girl was too cool to move faster than a saunter, too bad-ass to play defense or get a rebound, and I scored on her more than she liked and more than I should have.

She walked off the court after the game without a glance in my direction. Her boyfriend looked at me and said, "She's got an attitude. I don't really take her out in public much."

This, I thought, could be Tonya in a few years, ruined, a prisoner to the romance of wasted potential.

One night, sitting in the bleachers with Patty and Brittany's mom after a particularly bad practice with Tonya, I'd just made a joke about acquiring one of those *Wild Kingdom* tranquilizer guns to subdue certain of my players when Patty said, "Felicia gets in the car after practice and says, 'Mom, Tonya disrespects the coach.'"

She said it in Felicia's tone, shocked that such a thing could be possible.

"So I said to Felicia, I said, 'Let me tell you something. You ever pull some stunts like that, and the coach won't have to pull you out, because I'll do it for her, and then I'll beat you.'"

Brittany's mom piped in. "What's it going to be like when Tonya's thirteen? I tell you what it'll be like: *The Jerry Springer Show,* that's what. I always say, God, just don't let my kids be on *Springer.*"

"Okay?" Patty said, by way of agreement.

Avoiding *Springer* seemed a safe bet for Felicia, sane and cheerful as she was, but I wasn't so sure about Brittany. At the last practice, I'd overheard her threaten her mom, as she stood above Brittany trying to get her up off the floor, with a "kick in the privates."

A few days later, I ran into Brittany outside the gym. She was walking into practice with her head down, muttering something about "witnesses" and "proof," and I asked her what was up.

She started talking fast, saying she was being threatened at school by Tonya and Tonya's best friend, Danielle, who had a boyfriend, supposedly. According to this Danielle, Brittany had flirted with the supposed boyfriend, kicking him one day at lunch.

After hearing about Brittany's problems at school, I was more relieved than usual to see that Tonya was absent. We only had five players that night, and we began a one-on-one drill. The way the drill worked was, if the offensive player made a shot, it was a point for her. If the defensive player stole the ball or got a rebound or forced a travel, it was a point for her. If the offense got the rebound, it was another chance to score, and if the defense fouled, it was a point for the offense.

We'd been running the drill for five minutes when Brittany sat down on the floor and started crying. Her outburst couldn't have been basketball-related, because I'd been telling her she was doing well on the drill. She wouldn't say what was wrong, so I told her if she needed a break, that was fine, but she had to move off the court so the rest of us could continue. She scooted over approximately one inch, a move that reminded me very much of her nemesis Tonya. I tried out Patty's mother-look on her, and to my surprise, Brittany scooted her narrow behind out of bounds.

Brittany's mom had stepped out of the gym and missed all of this, but when she came back in, she made a beeline for her daughter. I don't know what the mom said, but Brittany was back playing in a few minutes.

Amanda was displaying her characteristic defensive footwork, which might have been appropriate for a boxer, but it had no business on a basketball court. She hopped, and what's more, she hopped backwards. For every inch her girl moved toward the basket, Amanda gave two.

My continuous preaching about planting feet and holding position hadn't stuck with Amanda. She was cooperative, I was sure of that, but I just hadn't found a way to make sense to her. Finally, I stopped the two girls and said, "Look here, Amanda, I want to show you something. Here's what you're doing on defense."

I had Emily try to score on me as I started hopping and moving backwards in what was a very accurate impression of Amanda's defense, if I do say so myself.

"Amanda, you're saying, 'Oh no, Emily, never mind me, you go on ahead, be my guest, don't let me hold you up.' "

I was a little relieved to see that Amanda could laugh at herself, especially if we all laughed at me.

"Now here's what you do instead," I said, planting my feet widely and signaling Emily to start over. "Emily's dribbling, she's moving to the hoop, right? She's working the ball, and Amanda's gonna say, 'You think you're gonna get by *me?*'" (I was incredulous at the idea.) " 'I don't *think* so!' "

Amanda and Emily laughed.

"You just say, 'No ma'am! You're gonna have to work *harder* than that. This is *my* house!' "

They were all giggling by then.

"Yeah, this is my house!" Beth hollered, jumping into the act like she was guarding me. "You get outta here, lady!"

She bumped me a little, stood back to gauge my response, stopping short of grabbing her crotch. "This is my property! You gotta pay me some rent!"

I was losing control of practice again, but that wasn't my primary concern. All I could think of was: *lady?*

I shook it off like a jammed finger.

"Yeah, that's right, Beth's got the idea." *Lady.*

Beth jumped back swaggering among the group, and maybe it was my imagination, but they all seemed to be standing a little taller.

The thing was, I didn't expect Amanda or Emily to talk like that. Hell, Amanda would barely talk at all, and Emily wouldn't look you in the eye. But they could think it, and that's all they really needed to do.

Tossing the ball to Emily, I said, "Okay, Amanda, let me see you plant your feet and hold your ground."

And she did it, just like I told her. But Emily was so much bigger, she used her behind to move Amanda even with her feet planted. Instead of hopping backwards, Amanda was being scooted backwards. We all laughed again, and I promised Amanda that it would work better in games, when she wasn't so outmatched in size. And I knew it would. I'd been scooted before myself.

Later, Amanda was on offense, dribbling with her eyes focused on the ball to the exclusion of all else, like she was playing the piano, which I'd been told she was very good at. I stopped her again and talked to her about keeping her head up, about maintaining a sense of her defender's position and taking advantage when her girl moved too far one way or the other. I took the ball and showed her, dribbling and waiting for my defender to go just a little too far, then switching hands and going the other way toward the hoop.

"Let's see it again," I said, tossing Amanda the ball. She started dribbling and moving around, doing a little better at keeping her eyes up, and I stood close. I watched, watched, watched until I saw Amanda's chance: her defender with a little too much weight on a foot, a little too much distance in the wrong direction. "Now!" I hollered, and she switched hands and went for the hoop. She looked astonished as she got close, and then she picked up her dribble and hesitated, giving her defender the split-second required to catch up. I explained that you had to shoot fast.

We stopped practice again after a few plays to show Amanda

exactly how to execute a rebound. I described the minutia of movement as another girl shot: turning around, getting my back on my girl, watching the ball to anticipate its direction, then going after it. When Amanda tried it, I kept my voice in her ears, saying, "Turn to the hoop, find your girl with your back, box her out, watch . . . watch . . . now run!"

With Amanda, you had to break things down, describe individual movements and tell her exactly what to do with different parts of her body. I had to do it the right way and the wrong way myself, tell her how to think even, then have her repeat a specific action several times, hoping she'd remember later when I wasn't talking her through it anymore.

Which she usually didn't. Even though she was bright, her brain just didn't operate that way. Working with her was like teaching a dyslexic person to read. It could be done, but it wasn't very easy.

After having spent half the season in athletic darkness, Amanda was pretty psyched about the lightbulbs going off in her head that night. When I told the team to go take a water break, Amanda said, "Can we keep going and do this some more? Please?"

It was impressive that the weakest player on the team wanted to keep doing an individual's drill that inevitably had her coming out last. When the other players said, "Yeah, let's do this some more," I told them we'd do it first thing next practice, but for now I wanted them to play some two-on-two, so we could work on passing.

Beth had to go home early, and when the others came back and we started to get teams together, there was a standoff. Allison, Emily, and Amanda stood beside each other, three against Brittany, making it clear they didn't want to play with her.

"Here's how we're going to do it," I said. "Tallest and shortest against the other two."

Allison, who was now on Brittany's team, said, "I don't want to play with someone who calls us all idiots." I hadn't heard Brittany call anyone names, so I didn't say much. I just told them that's what we had, so let's get going.

As we played, Brittany treated everyone with a mixture of haughty disdain and illogical cruelty available only to those with very good bone structure. She was putting the smack-down on Amanda, standing too close, doing her best to tower and look down on her, bumping chests a little, acting like some kind of beautiful thug.

Once, Brittany got Amanda stuck dribbling with her head down at half-court. I had my fancy whistle out, playing ref, and I watched closely, dying to call a foul and help Amanda out. But Brittany wasn't fouling, just driving Amanda nuts.

All of a sudden, Amanda picked up her dribble and looked over at me, shouting, "Brittany said she was prettier than me!"

I had the two of them stop the play and come back to the top of the key, and before they started again, I said, "Brittany, is that true?"

She hesitated, looking at me and visibly debating with herself about whether or not to tell the truth. "Yes," she finally admitted, a little ashamed and exceedingly miserable.

She must have been whispering some kind of crazy spells, because as close as I was watching, I hadn't heard. "Now listen to me," I said to Brittany. "We don't need that kind of hatefulness, and you're going to stop disrespecting your teammates if you want to play on this team."

We kept playing. Brittany backed off Amanda, at least a little.

Leaving the gym that night, I asked Brittany's mom about the incident at school, and the mom was immediately angry, describing Tonya's friend Danielle as a "little nothing," and saying she was just like Tonya and nobody liked her. The mom sounded like a kid herself, like she'd been there and was part of the soap opera.

"I told Brittany they were only picking on her because they were jealous. Because she has friends and people like her."

Something sounded off. It was a hesitation somewhere, a flicker in the eye, and I was hit with an image of the mom telling Brittany that Tonya was jealous, not because Brittany had friends, but because she was pretty. It was strange how clearly I saw it, like getting a quick scene from a cable channel you don't subscribe to.

I thought about Tonya. The last time I'd seen her had been the day I'd given her a ride home. Chatting away, she'd told me it was okay if I took her out of the games now, because her dad had explained things to her, telling her that I only took her out because she was one of my best players, and coaches had to make sure their stars got some rest and were able to play at the end of the game.

You can't blame a ten-year-old for accepting an irresistible possibility forced down her throat by parents. I'm gifted, says one, I'm beautiful, says the other, game over. Maybe that's what made them both a little crazy, an understanding that under any circumstances, they were expected not to be ordinary.

We'd met every team in the league, and now we were starting over, scheduled to play the team that had trounced us our first game. We had a winning record, and we were confident and faced games calmly.

Tonya's stepmom called me one hour before the game and told me Tonya wouldn't be coming that day, and probably not for the rest of the season, because she'd gotten in trouble for fighting.

It was obvious that my role in Tonya's family drama was to be the distraught coach who found it impossible to win a game without the presence of their gifted little athlete.

"Well," I said lightly, "tell her to act right, so she can come back and play." Then I laughed like it was no big deal.

Brittany jumped up and down with happiness when she found out Tonya was gone. She smiled at everyone, apparently willing to be friends with ugly idiots again.

As we huddled before the buzzer, I talked to them about number five, the one who had scored all the lay-ups on us the first game. I hurriedly told them to help Beth out if Five got past her, but I knew it was a tall order. In fourth grade, it was a challenge to remember to get your own man, much less keep an eye on someone else's.

The game was close, but late in the first half Beth was out while Five was in, and we got a little behind. I went over to Beth and gave her a politician speech again. "This is our toughest period. We're just trying to hang in there for now. We'll catch back up next period, when *you're* back in."

We were down by five at halftime. I gathered the girls around and told them we had some catching up to do, but there was time. We were definitely not stalling now, and if they had a good shot, they should take it. But only a good shot, I said.

Four minutes later, we were three behind, and four minutes after that, we were only one behind. It appeared, as long as Beth was in the game, the Ball Hawgs had the edge. Between the sixth and seventh periods, I said to the girls, "Okay, look, we're making progress and catching up. Do you feel it?"

I could tell they did.

Little did I know at the time that we were playing the notorious New School, where the rich kids went. All the Ball Hawg parents knew about the New School team from the previous seasons. Their coach, a woman, practiced her girls every day in PE class. Word was, she demanded the impossible out of her players, and usually got it, and she'd even been thrown out of a few games for bad behavior. All I knew was the other team was well coached, calling plays, setting screens to shake Beth so number five could score lay-ups.

They were seriously competent ten-year-old basketball players, but we were no slouches. Even Emily, normally so spacy and timid, was getting her share of jump balls and rebounds.

The game stayed within a point in either direction into the last four-minute period, when number five, going for a rebound, tripped and fell to the floor with a loud thud. The gym got quiet as everyone watched to see how bad it was, then someone screamed from the bleachers: "Suck it up, Lindsey!"

The voice belonged to a tough-looking woman, apparently Lindsey's mother, who ran onto the court and started telling the girl to get herself back in the game right now, but Lindsey just wailed louder. She was hurt, she was out, and as she walked past me leaving the court, I said good game, hoping she'd heard.

We hung on to our one-point lead like a last dollar. With two minutes left, we had the ball, and I called my timeout. Let's be quiet. Look at the score. Look at the clock. Think.

"No bad shots," I told them. "Let's get in there and maintain our lead, and be very selective with your shots. Do you understand? What did I just say?"

They did it, stalling for a minute, taking a good shot, and scoring. We won by three, and the parents swarmed, gleeful at this win in particular. Beth, wearing her usual postgame red apple face, gave me the lowdown on the New School and their coach.

"She talks so mean to her players . . . she's all like, 'What are you *thinking*?! What are you *doing?*'" Beth frowned and moved her arms in the jerky motions coaches use when they ask those questions. "She yells at them all the time, and her players don't like her. They're all like, 'She's crazy,' and 'She needs to chill out,' and 'What's her problem?'"

I said to Beth, "Well, I yell sometimes, too."

She looked at me a second and said, "Oh, you don't have it in you to be mean."

I guess even a ten-year-old can know the difference between assertive and aggressive, and here I was in my thirties, still figuring out how to give myself permission not to hold what was real in check. I was glad it wasn't too late to be learning that.

Brittany was hateful as a molting snake during the next practice, while everyone else was excited to do the one-on-one drill again. After we finished the drill and had a short break, I lined the girls up according to height to get teams and matchups for three-on-three. This was a mistake, because it meant that Brittany was guarding poor Amanda again.

Going up the court for our first play, Brittany yelled, "I hate this! This is so stupid! I hate basketball!" She was looking at Beth when she said it, trying to get her buy-in. I was grateful when Beth hollered back, "Why'd you sign up then?"

When they headed back down the court toward the bleachers where the parents sat, Brittany gave Amanda a sneaky shove out of bounds when I had my head turned. Beth's mother screamed from her position in the stands, "Brittany! Don't push people! You can't just shove people into bleachers!"

Have you ever dated someone who drove you insane, and then, all of a sudden, while you're in the shower or driving or trying to work, you realize, *Hey, he's just an a-hole, it's really not that complicated?* I had a similar epiphany regarding Brittany.

I stayed close to Brittany and Amanda, holding my whistle inches from my mouth, telling Brittany she could not *touch* the person she was guarding. Brittany continued to confuse the game of basketball with a wrestling beauty contest, but we avoided serious injury.

After several more trips up and down the floor, I told them to go get a drink. I wanted to think a minute and shore up my patience.

When they came back, I took them to the other side of the court, away from the parents, and we began working on defense. I tossed Allison the ball as I got set to guard her, thinking about what it was that Brittany did wrong, and trying to tell them all how not to do it without singling Brittany out.

"Look," I said, "when we're playing defense, we don't have to run all around our girl like this."

As Allison dribbled, I played defense on her like a cat being teased by a toy.

"All we have to do is stay between our player and the goal, okay? Don't go all crazy, just stay in control, and watch your girl's midsection to anticipate which way she might go. That's it. Stay between her and the goal. Watch the belly. No running around all over the place."

They sat in a circle, smiling a little, relaxed and in the mood to be entertained. Except for Brittany, still bristling with defiant exile.

"Remember what we've said about keeping your knees bent and one hand up? That's what I want to see. Easy, right? Who's got it?"

Emily's hand shot up, barely beating out Amanda's.

"Come on, Emily, and I see you, Amanda. You'll be next."

Emily stood up and guarded me, perfectly. So the rest of the team would pay attention and not begin acting like a litter of hyena puppies, and to gather all the good feeling and solidarity I could, I had them watch and critique each other.

"Tell me what you see, team. Are Emily's knees bent?"

They nodded and said yes here and there.

"Is she between me and the goal? Is she fouling me?"

They watched, evaluating Emily's defense like professionals, and they agreed she was doing everything right.

"All right then. Good job, Emily."

I touched Emily's hand in a low-level high-five that wouldn't make us both feel like dorks. Brittany rolled her eyes.

"Come on, Amanda, let's go."

Amanda jumped up and guarded me. I asked the team all the questions about her, and she passed their test.

"Now, what's she gonna do if I make the mistake of putting the ball in front of her?"

I dribbled high and wrong in front of Amanda, and she stole it from me.

"That's right," I said. "She's gonna take it from me." Give me five, friend.

One by one, everyone got her turn, until Brittany was the only player left. I'd made it so easy for her to become part of the group again and be liked and accepted and learn something, to be forgiven and move on. All she had to do was try, just a little.

But you know, I guess she might have felt like I did that time when I was in therapy, when Wanda had asked me if I was really ready to change. Or when I'd asked Tonya about having a good time that first practice and she wouldn't just say yes like everyone else. Sometimes people just have issues, and there's nothing you can do about it.

Brittany stood in front of us and acted like a corpse.

"Come on, sweetie," I said. "Bend your knees, straighten your back, let's go."

If it's possible to play defense sarcastically, she managed it, and with all my diplomacy shunned, I had no choice but to follow through.

"All right, team, what do you see? Are her knees bent? Are her hands up? Is she between me and the goal?"

They waved their hands dismissively and shook their heads. Felicia held her nose and moved a hand in front of her face as if something stank. Brittany looked at them like *they* stank.

A few weeks earlier, we'd worked on taking the ball out of bounds, and I'd put myself on Brittany. As she got ready to pass the ball in, I spontaneously acted like a crazed defender, jumping up and down like my feet were on fire. I just did it, without thinking about it, to be stupid and try to get everyone relaxed about being guarded. Brittany looked surprised for a second, like I'd startled her, and then she started giggling so hard I thought she might fall down. When she finally stopped laughing, her lovely face was lit with delight, and she looked at me like a baby enchanted with my peekaboo.

How was it that now she hated me so much?

It really was complicated, but I decided it wasn't up to me to figure it out. Instead, later that week, I made a call to Brittany's *Springer*-averse mom. Before the next game, which was our last one, Brittany approached me and said she was "sorry for having a bad attitude." I said it was okay, and let's just try to do better. I squeezed one of her shoulders as she hugged me around the waist and her mother looked on.

During our warm-up, Brittany didn't talk to anyone, and no one was talking to her. When we got in our circle for the usual last-minute stuff, I decided to try something different and change the vibe. I asked them, "Remember what we said the very first practice we had? Remember what our goal was for the season?"

"Get the ball inside!" several of them shouted.

"That's our goal on offense," I said, "but does anyone remember what we said we were gonna do the very first time we practiced?"

"Have fun!" a few of them remembered.

"That's right," I said. "Let's try to get back to that, okay? Let's play hard, but let's have a good time, too, okay?"

They were smiling. Everything felt a little better.

We began playing, and then Brittany did something so evil and subversive, she managed to shock me some more. That little Attila the Hun in lip-gloss hollered for the pass, as always, and when she got it, she slung the ball in any direction without even looking for a teammate. She was throwing the ball away in one big "screw you": screw you, ugly idiotic teammates . . . screw you, stupid coach . . . screw you, basketball . . . screw you, Mom.

Beth yelled at her, understanding that Brittany couldn't possibly play this badly without trying. She stopped passing to her, and I hastily revised my lineup to take Brittany out the next period and minimize her playing time.

The other team had two short guards who made all their points. After a few periods, I took Felicia and Amanda off them and put Emily and Beth on them instead. On the first timeout after the switch, Emily kept her girl under control, and Beth got all over the star point guard, forcing a turnover. We went down and scored, and I felt bad for what I was about to do.

From the sidelines, I said, as quietly as I could, "Beth . . . what you're doing up there, it's working . . . keep it up."

I had the ruthless job of telling Beth to shut down that hard-working guard, and all I could do in the name of decency was remain somewhat somber about it. I tried not to make it too obvious, what was going on and how unseemly it was, a grown woman going in for the kill like that, and that made the process kosher, if no less ugly.

Beth nodded. She got another steal, and the guard began to crumble. During an eight-point run, every time we went down on defense, I'd say, "Do it again, Beth, do it again."

We won by twelve, and when the final buzzer sounded, Brittany jumped up and down, enjoying the victory she'd tried to sabotage. I watched our season end and felt a little sick at seeing the short guard walk off with her head down. But you know, that's the way basketball is. It's just gonna break your heart sometimes.

Overtime

YEARS HAVE GONE BY. Whole Saturday afternoons lost on a court are reality only in my memory. And here's the big news: I have a son. His name is Jackson, he's two, and he's funny and nice and I think you'd like him.

Now I take Jackson to the playground, and we'll watch a game. I squat down beside him on the sidelines, and his chubby waist strains lightly against my arms. He wants in, and I want in, too, but we settle for watching. He reaches impossibly for the ball. I laugh at the jokes, whisper my *uhhh-huhh* and *there you go* and other quiet approvals, sometimes shake my head a little and think, *You better take that.*

I play when I can, but the court no longer pulls me. Like an old lover you've gotten over as much as you're going to, the game is bittersweet to me now, not urgent.

Maybe it's true that, what's important to you, like any person in this whole world, can only love you imperfectly. I'm trying to get better at all the different kinds of love, learning to navigate them a little more skillfully, sometimes like a snarl of city highways, and sometimes like a long dirt road without a sign for miles. I know I'm succeeding when I feel that old clarity that was always there when the game was good, those blessed moments pulled from the chaos when you see what matters and nothing else.

I guess it's just as well that things begin to leave you behind and what you have left is the memory, existing in your mind-as-time-machine, hauled out and relived like the swish of a perfect shot. After years on the court, so many players occupy my brain in the broad, blurry regions of type. The up-and-coming serious shorties. Overweight guys with the energy-efficient grace of dancing elephants. Prissy tennis pros. Trash talkers. Old guys with their patented shots. Ladies' men. Squint-eyed racists. Shirtless college boys. Glowering girls, and girls who get into games with smiles.

That's where most players go, but then there are a few who exist in esoteric folds and creases with unexpected associates. Beth—blond, white, southern—slides along a goofy groove with black, urban Rolando, both reveling in their ridiculous antics and ability to make friends. My favorite ref is somewhere else, working peacefully beside the good teacher dude at Westwood Park, the one who pushed you but not too far. One says little and one never stops talking, yet both make it their business to teach.

And in a place of comfort and hope, David and his mom still play together. He forever feels taller when she looks at him, even though I know, back in Chicago, he has gotten old enough to slump and scowl and give her trouble. Nearby, Felicia's mother Patty still shows me there's a time to hug and a time to turn away, and a California family forever kicks a ball in the park.

Little homeless Xavier has a place, too, in a pool of sorrow deeper than ever now that I know something about all a child needs. I didn't help him. I hope somebody did.

I still feel, sometimes, the old desire to dive into forgetting. I still crave, now and again, to be free, flying, with no one to stop me. But that dream comes less often now as I take more seriously the possibility that we're all in charge of creating a reality. Like everyone, I have something to teach. Just by navigating those roads, someone will see, someone will learn. Maybe that's how it always was, on all those Saturday afternoons lost on the court, as I looked for what I didn't know I needed, and watched people, and never really thought too much about how someone might be watching me back.

I wouldn't pretend to have the answer to Plato and Clem's argument about where talent comes from, if you're born with it or if you get it by working hard. What I do know about talent is that it's characterized by ease. As Steve at Never Too Late might say, I know what talent *looks* like. Some people are talented at love. And maybe love *is* easy for some people. Like basketball, it hasn't been for me, still isn't, but being remembered is important to me now, even by someone I don't know, maybe *especially* by someone I don't know, someone who was just shooting around, waiting to see what would happen next.

And so I'll keep trying to show my son—and anyone else who might be watching—some of the moves I picked up on the court; tricky balances of resilience and flexibility, courage and serenity, confidence and humility, moving and stillness. I'll try to represent always looking for the open man. And love, the kind that makes you feel taller, the kind that remains even when you're by yourself. Most of all, I'll try to teach him that.